THE NEW BEST OF FINE WOODWORKING

Designing & Building
Cabinets

Designing & Building
Cabinets

The Editors of
Fine Woodworking

The Taunton Press

The Taunton Press
Inspiration for hands-on living®

The Taunton Press, Inc., 63 South Main Street, PO Box 5506, Newtown, CT 06470-5506
e-mail: tp@taunton.com

Distributed by Publishers Group West

Jacket/Cover design: Susan Fazekas
Interior design: Susan Fazekas
Layout: Carol Petro
Front cover photographer: Asa Christiana, courtesy *Fine Woodworking*
Back cover photographers: (top left, bottom right) Anatole Burkin, courtesy
Fine Woodworking; (top right) Strother Purdy, courtesy *Fine Woodworking*

The New Best of Fine Woodworking® is a trademark of The Taunton Press, Inc.,
registered in the U.S. Patent and Trademark Office.

Library of Congress Cataloging-in-Publication Data

Designing & building cabinets / the editors of Fine woodworking.
     p. cm. -- (The new best of fine woodworking)
  ISBN 1-56158-732-X
  1. Kitchen cabinets. 2. Cabinetwork. I. Fine woodworking. II. Series.
  TT197.5.K57D47 2004
  684.1'6--dc22

                              2004006983

Printed in the United States of America
10 9 8 7 6 5 4 3 2 1

The following manufacturers/names appearing in *Designing & Building Cabinets* are trademarks:
Accuride®, Avonite®, Baldwin®, Ball and Ball®, Bessey® K-Body, Bibralter®, Brusso®, Capitol
Hardware®, Capsray®, Corian®, Dustfoe® 66, Formica®, Fountainhead®, Genie® Lift, Grass®
1006, Hafele™, Home Depot®, Jesada®, Lamello®, Liberty Hardware®, Medite®, Merit®,
Micarta®, Benjamin Moore IronClad®, National Particleboard Association℠, Plum Creek®,
Robertson®, Sam Maloof®, Sherwin-Williams®, Surell®, 3M®, Twinfast®, Virutex®,
Whitechapel®, Wilsonart®, Woodcraft®, X-Acto®.

Working wood is inherently dangerous. Using hand or power tools improperly or ignoring
safety practices can lead to permanent injury or even death. Don't try to perform operations
you learn about here (or elsewhere) unless you're certain they are safe for you. If something
about an operation doesn't feel right, don't do it. Look for another way. We want you to
enjoy the craft, so please keep ssafety foremost in your mind whenever you're in the shop.

Acknowledgments

Special thanks to the authors, editors,
art directors, copy editors, and other
staff members of *Fine Woodworking*
who contributed to the development
of the articles in this book.

Contents

Introduction

Rare is the woodworker who has never built a cabinet. Sure, there are those who specialize in chairs, or carving, or turning, but at some point most of us who work wood have made a cabinet. Cabinets are among the most useful of pieces. They hold all manner of stuff: books, clothes, dishes, food, and more. Without cabinets, our homes would be in disarray, a massive jumble of our personal possessions.

I have certainly built more cabinets than any other form of furniture. My last kitchen remodel alone required about 10 cabinets. It taught me a lot about working efficiently and staying organized.

Cabinets may be built of all types of materials—plywood, particleboard, solid wood, or any combination. You can make them as basic or elaborate as you wish, sometimes too elaborate. A few years ago, Kevin Ireton, the editor of *Fine Homebuilding* magazine, watched as I struggled in the *Fine Woodworking* workshop to build a pair of veneered curved doors for a large armoire destined to store clothing. Noting the amount of time it was taking me to build the piece, he commented: "Wouldn't it be easier to just build another closet?" He was right, of course, but woodworkers don't get into the craft because they want an easy solution. We want to build pieces that serve us well, but they must also add to the beauty of our homes.

Whether you need to build one cabinet or a roomful, the articles collected here will walk you through all facets of cabinetmaking. From selecting materials to planning and design, and on to construction of the cases, doors, and drawers, these articles, from the pages of *Fine Woodworking* magazine, offer a variety of approaches and styles.

There's an adage about closet space and how you never have enough. Well, I think the same is true of cabinetry. Let this book be your guide.

Anatole Burkin
Editor
Fine Woodworking

Making Big Cabinets Manageable

BY NIALL BARRETT

THE AUTHOR USES small parts and knockdown hardware for his cabinets. Parts easily fit inside his standard minivan.

orking in New York City, where most of my clients live, is trying even at the best of times. There's rarely ever a place to park, so I end up double-parking to unload a delivery, always keeping a sharp eye out for the police. After that, I'm forced to pay exorbitant fees to park my van in a lot. Freight elevators tend to be small and poorly located, and stairways have sharp corners to negotiate. I once delivered a cabinet that would not fit in the elevator, so I had to walk it up two flights of stairs. I was lucky the client didn't live on the 35th floor. Doors and hallways can be quite narrow when you're trying to deliver a large cabinet.

These anxiety-provoking restrictions and horror stories from fellow cabinetmakers are what started me thinking about cabinets in a new way. It became clear to me that smaller parts were the answer. They would be easier to handle and transport. The challenge would be to assemble them quickly and not have the end result look like a jigsaw puzzle of small pieces. These days, I routinely build large pieces, like the stand-alone television cabinet shown below, in

Television Cabinet, One Piece at a Time

For author Niall Barrett, getting a new custom cabinet from his shop in upstate New York to a client's house many miles away is all in a day's work. Many of the cabinets he makes, like the television cabinet in the photos at right, go in pieces and are assembled on the spot with knockdown hardware.

At the site, the author sets the base ❶, adds two lower carcases ❷, attaches finished side pieces ❸, and, finally, adds the top, door and hardware ❹. Elapsed time is approximately four hours.

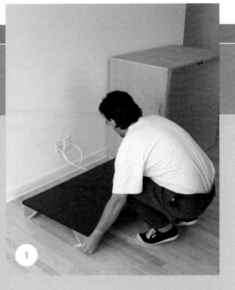

No matter how you decide to break a job into smaller pieces, the trick is putting it all together so it looks like a unified whole.

Knockdown Fasteners for Small Components

Knockdown hardware offers the strength and durability of more permanent fasteners but allows a cabinet to be taken apart and moved as easily as it was assembled. There are many types of knockdown, or ready-to-assemble, hardware. Here are the author's favorites.

HEX-DRIVE CONNECTOR BOLTS

These are bolts with a machine thread, usually 1/4-20, and large, flat heads that you tighten with an Allen wrench (see the top photo below). I team them up with threaded inserts for right-angle joints, shelves, and dividers. I also use the inserts to attach crown and base assemblies to cabinet cases.

These bolts also come with matching threaded sleeves. I use them for fastening the sides of two cabinet carcases to one another (see the bottom photo). The standard finish is an antique bronze color. But you can also buy these bolts in black, or you can spray paint them any color that you like. A number of suppliers sell these bolts and sleeves. I usually buy mine at either Woodcraft® or Liberty Hardware®.

HEX-DRIVE CONNECTOR BOLTS AND THREADED INSERTS **fasten cabinet parts together where connector heads can be exposed. The connector (see the photo at right) secures a cabinet carcase to its base.**

HEX-DRIVE CONNECTOR BOLTS AND THREADED SLEEVES **are ideal for linking adjoining carcases.**

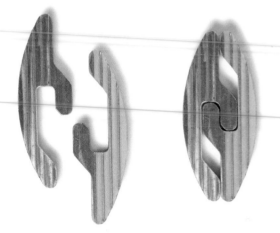

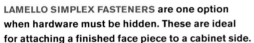

LAMELLO SIMPLEX FASTENERS are one option when hardware must be hidden. These are ideal for attaching a finished face piece to a cabinet side.

LAMELLO SIMPLEX KD FASTENERS

These fasteners come as interlocking aluminum parts to be glued into regular biscuit slots. They are used in pairs. I often use this hardware to join flat pieces edge to edge and at 90° angles to one another. The hardware is invisible once installed. I used them to join the finished side panels over the cabinet carcases in the installation shown in the photo at right.

Epoxy glue works best for installation, although I have had some success using polyurethane glue for light applications where the joint is not under much stress from weight or tension. Lamello® makes a tool intended to simplify installation. I buy the fasteners and the insertion tool from Select Machinery.

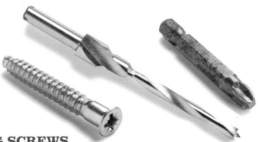

CONFIRMAT SCREWS can be inserted and removed many times without sacrificing holding power. They require a special bit and driver.

CONFIRMAT CONNECTING SCREWS

These connecting screws (see the photos above) have a deep thread with no taper. To use them, you must also buy a special step drill bit for piloting the workpieces, as shown in the photo at right. You can use these screws to put a cabinet together and to take it apart again a number of times with no loss of holding power. You can buy these screws with small heads, designed to be countersunk, or with large, flat heads like those of hex-drive connector bolts. I only use the ones with small heads.

Also, you need a special driver bit called a Pozidrive. It looks a lot like a standard Phillips head, but it fits and grabs better in the head of the screw. A Phillips bit will strip the head of the screw if you drive it home with a lot of torque. Outwater Hardware sells the screws and bits.

Sources

Liberty Hardware
800-542-3789

Outwater Hardware
800-631-0342

Select Machinery
800-789-2323

Woodcraft
800-225-1153

easily handled components. When I get to a job site, whether it's in New York City or elsewhere, I assemble the pieces with knockdown hardware.

This approach is not just for woodworkers who make deliveries to a large city. It also works for the guy building a large pantry cabinet in his garage who will have to move it through the house into the kitchen.

Make Cabinets Easy to Finish and Move

Small components are light and easy to move around the workroom and take up less space at every step of the way. For me, that's important because I work in a fairly small shop in the basement of my house. The ceilings are less than 8 ft. off the floor. I often build units that are too large to put together in my shop; they aren't fully as-sembled until they are delivered to the site.

Whether you use stain, oil, varnish, or a sprayed lacquer topcoat, finishes are easy to apply when you work with small compo-nents and flat panels. There are no corners to collect excess stain, primer, or topcoat, so the finish looks more even. Also, by work-ing with flat panels, you can get a lot more finishing done by spraying pieces vertically. They take up less floor space than finished cabinets, so I can spray more at one time. And by spraying flat panels vertically, they collect less dust as they dry. This can be sig-nificant because I usually use a water-based finish, which takes longer to dry than nitro-cellulose lacquer.

You can fit an incredibly large volume of material into a small truck or van if the project is broken down into flat or small pieces (see the photo on p. 4). This alone can save a few hundred dollars for the rental of a large truck and the time it takes to pick it up and return it. Oh yes, the other benefit I enjoy is the amazed look on the client's face after the collection of parts I delivered is almost magically transformed into a beautiful piece of furniture.

Plan Ahead for Components and Fasteners

When I'm in the design phase, I start by thinking about how a piece can be broken down into smaller, more manageable parts and how I'll put it together again. I deter-mine, for example, whether a cabinet with a center divider and two doors can be made as two cabinets. Or I'll weigh the advan-tages of making the crown and the base as separate components rather than perma-nently fastening them to the case in the shop. I make a quick sketch, an exploded view of the individual parts, to see whether it makes sense to build something that way. Detailed drawings can follow later.

Once I've determined which route to take, I think about design elements that make the job go more smoothly and the piece look better when it's done. Knock-down hardware makes strong connections between cabinet parts, but it can be difficult to make two surfaces align perfectly along the length of a joint. To solve this problem, I sometimes add a spacer between cabinets and set it back slightly from the edge. This creates a shadow line at the joint and makes the seam less obvious. For the same reason, it's usually better to offset one hard surface from another, like the seam where a bed rail joins the corner post.

No matter how you decide to break a job into smaller pieces, the trick is putting it all together so it looks like a unified whole. And that's where the hardware shown on pp. 6-7 comes in.

NIALL BARRETT owns and operates Avalon Studios, a custom cabinetmaking shop in Narrowsburg, New York.

A Game Plan
for Big Cabinet Jobs

Over the years, I've built close to 20 libraries for residential clients. To me, these rooms of cabinet-work and millwork are interesting for their variety. A library—more than any other room in a house—brings together a lot of different components. Case work, shelving, drawers and pull-outs, frame-and-panel doors, glass doors, paneling, and unique moldings all make up the finished job. Case

work may vary from simple bookcases to more elaborate storage units for television and audio equipment. But in the end, they're all just plywood boxes dressed up to look good.

For a large and complicated job like this one (see the photo below), I always measure the room twice, on two separate days, to reduce the chance of making a mistake in laying out and sizing the work. By

BY JOHN W. WEST

ON ANY JOB, particularly those that are large and complicated, accurate measuring can mean the difference between success and failure.

checking the two sets of measurements against one another, any discrepancy will show up readily and may have to be resolved with a third visit to the job site. I used story poles (scraps of lumber on which all the job-site conditions are marked) for many years because they're almost foolproof. But lately, I've developed another system that works more efficiently for me.

To lay out and design a room like this one, I start with a set of drawings from the architect that have been approved by the clients. The drawings show scaled elevations, or front views, of how they want the room to look. To figure out exactly how cabinets and paneling and moldings will all fit together, I use those drawings to make my own in a larger scale based on the measurements taken at the site. From my first set of drawings, I make another set of free-hand shop sketches where I figure out the joinery details and the actual cut size in overall dimensions of every cabinet, door, wall panel and piece of molding that will

make up the job. From those shop sketches, I make cut lists that show every piece of plywood or lumber by finished size— thickness, width, and length—and the number of pieces of each. There are still many times when I will draw out some details full-sized, especially when I deal with angles or curves or I want to be sure something is going to look right.

Choosing Materials and Tuning Up Equipment

For all open bookcases and wall and door panels, my shop buys the best quality (an A-1 grade), sequence-matched, veneer-core plywood. I stay away from particleboard and fiberboard cores. I'm getting too old to hoist the extra weight. We use ¾-in.-thick material for all the case work parts and large panels, ½ in. for smaller wall panels and flat door panels, and ¼-in. (A-3 grade) plywood for cabinet backs and drawer bottoms (see the photos on the facing page). We make everything else, including drawer cases,

Layout and design

SEVERAL STAGES OF PAPERWORK.
From an architect's original drawing, the author makes a large-scale version. Next come shop sketches, a parts list, and full-sized details.

from solid lumber. By using sequenced-matched panels, we get the same color and grain patterns throughout the room. For cases that are sunken into a closet alcove or hidden by doors, we use a lesser shop-grade plywood (costing about half as much as the A-1 panels) because the cases are not seen, and you can still get a similar color once they are stained and finished.

Before we start a project like this, we perform a major tune-up on all the equipment (see the sidebar on p. 12). The time spent on tune-up is critical because one thing we do that's different from many cabinet shops is cut all the plywood and mill all the lumber for a given job before assembling any cabinets. That means shelves and door stiles and drawer parts are all machined and cut to size before case work or paneling goes together. The machining has to be accurate.

We change knives on the jointer and the planer and reset the thickness gauges to be accurate within a tolerance of less than $\frac{1}{100}$ in. We also install freshly sharpened blades on the saws. All the machines are calibrated to agree with one designated tape measure we'll use throughout the job.

When we cut plywood sheet stock, we always cut off the factory edges, usually taking at least an inch from all sides. We may not cut as much off the long edges, but we always remove at least an inch from the ends because they are sanded over and thinner than the center of the panel. The sanding machines at plywood factories often leave a pronounced bevel on the ends (sometimes even sanding through the face veneer). Also, edges are often torn up from handling, and you cannot count on the corners being square. Unless you have a panel saw, you may have to spend some extra effort making a jig to guarantee square corners when you cut up the plywood (see the sidebar on p. 13). It's worth the time.

Materials

PLYWOOD FOR PANELS AND CASE WORK. The 18 cases and scores of panels that went into this library required 45 sheets of veneer-core plywood of varying grades and thicknesses.

A-1 grade, ¾ in.
Sequence-matched sheets used for large wall panels and most of the cases.

A-1 grade, ½ in.
Also sequence-matched, used for small wall panels and flat door panels.

A-3 grade, ¼ in.
Good one side only, used for cabinet backs and drawer bottoms.

Shop grade, ¾ in. (not shown)
Plywood with one good face, used where panels are less prominent, like a cabinet interior. Shop-grade ply costs about half as much as premium-grade plywood but can be stained and finished for a close match.

Tune Up Your Tools

To get off on the right foot, make sure tools have sharp knives, and choose a single tape measure for the job.

One tape, start to finish

Tape measures aren't all the same. Using one tape, what the author calls a master tape, ensures accuracy in cutting cabinet parts. For quick identification, the author scratches a symbol into the tape's case (like the triangle on this one), so it won't be confused with any other tape.

Change and set planer knives

After installing a sharp set of knives, the author sets them with a gauge. The process is fast, and knives are accurate to within a few thousandths of an inch.

Calibrate table saw rip fence

Using a scrap piece of plywood, the author checks the rip fence setting against the master tape. The table saw should be checked again with each blade change.

Jointer

New jointer knives are set flush to the outfeed table. Table surfaces are cleaned and waxed and checked for alignment. Depth-of-cut gauge is reset if necessary.

Shaper knives

The author grinds his own shaper knives for all of the molding that must go into a job. He sharpens previously made knives and sets them aside for quick access.

Factory Fresh Doesn't Mean It's Square

You cannot trust that any sheet of plywood from the factory will have square corners, and you cannot make square cabinets with out-of-square parts.

Before I owned a panel saw, I worked in a shop where we used a jig over a regular cabinet saw fence, like the one shown below, for squaring up sheet goods. By tacking an additional straightedge to one edge of the plywood (left) and running it under the jig (right), we were able—simply and fairly quickly—to square up sheets of plywood.

When I'm getting ready to make the plywood cuts for a job at hand, I look through the sheets for the important pieces, the ones that will be most prominent. I rough cut those pieces first, a little bigger than the final size, to make them more manageable. I also make any necessary repetitive cuts of similarly sized pieces, like base cabinet sides. It's better to crosscut first and rip last, so I cut all those oversized pieces to the finished length first. To guarantee that you get square corners on all your plywood pieces, always place a freshly cut edge against the fence with each new cut, until all four sides have been trimmed off.

1 Clamp the jig to the saw fence with the outside of the sawblade flush with the edge of the jig. Tack a straightedge onto the workpiece to a square line marked in pencil.

2 Run the workpiece through the saw, keeping even pressure on the straightedge against the jig.

3 Leave plenty of space between the blade and saw fence to prevent the offcut from binding.

Build for the Outside Dimension of the Box

With the cases we build, all the horizontal pieces are let into the verticals by the full thickness of the material, usually ¾ in., in either rabbet or dado joints (see the drawing on the facing page). One important chore that rabbets and dadoes do is to locate things. And your biggest enemy in making boxes is the assembly time. The machining and preparation of all the parts is worth the extra time it takes when you get to assembly. Jobs will go together better, faster, easier, squarer and truer. Anything that you can do that helps you to index or locate parts for assembly, the better off you are, especially if you are working alone.

If there's a place where we need additional support or a means of keeping a box straight, we put in additional pieces we call spreaders (see the drawing on the facing page). The tops of base cabinets serve as spreaders and also provide a way of fastening a counter from underneath. If there is a fascia piece, which serves as a background for cornice molding, above the solid top of an open bookcase, then we'll put spreaders across the top.

For cases like a kitchen cabinet, where you have a recessed toe kick, we notch out the sides of the cabinet and add a spreader or two as a nailing surface for the toe kickboard. In cabinets where there is a baseboard across the bottom of the cabinet, we may add one or two spreaders to stiffen the bottom of the cabinet and to act as nailers for the baseboard. All spreaders, no matter where they are, are always let into a dado the same depth as the cabinet top and bottom or a fixed shelf.

We cut a ⅜-in. by ⅜-in. rabbet to affix the ¼-in. back to the cabinet. When cabinets go against a wall with bulges in it, that extra ⅛ in. of space usually provides enough clearance so that the cabinets will go flat to the wall.

We use an overhead router to cut all our plywood joints because it's easier to control the overall dimension of cases. Overhead routing leaves a consistent thickness of material in plywood parts because the router bit is fixed in space above the work surface as the plywood is run underneath it. Routing with a hand router is the opposite: The depth of cut remains the same, but the final width of the case work will vary with different thicknesses in the plywood. You can make an overhead router from scraps of plywood; it's not that hard. Or you can simply measure the thickness of each piece of plywood and adjust the depth of the router cut accordingly, but the job will take more time that way.

We cut a full rabbet, about ¼ in. deep, depending on the actual thickness of the plywood, for all the top and bottom pieces. We also cut matching dadoes for any fixed shelves. We developed this system for two reasons: strength and accuracy. I'm convinced that having the horizontal pieces sitting on a rabbeted or dadoed ledge at full-thickness makes a stronger joint. And by using the overhead router with the cutting depth set to leave exactly ½ in. of material after the cut is made, we can always trust that the overall outside dimension of the cabinet will be accurate. It doesn't matter that the ¾-in. plywood we ordered actually came from the factory anywhere from ¹¹⁄₁₆ in. to ²⁵⁄₃₂ in. thick, as it sometimes does. By building to the outside dimensions of boxes, we can control the overall length of a string of connected boxes. We have put together strings of six or seven large cases and have been off less than ¹⁄₁₆ in. for spans of more than 20 ft.

Simple Plywood Boxes

Floor-to-ceiling bookcase

Cabinets for this library were built to store books, audio and video equipment, a large television, and glassware for a wet bar. Although some of the details (doors and face frames) and all of the sizes varied, the cases were all made using the same basic construction methods for ¾-in. plywood parts.

Kitchen-type bar cabinet

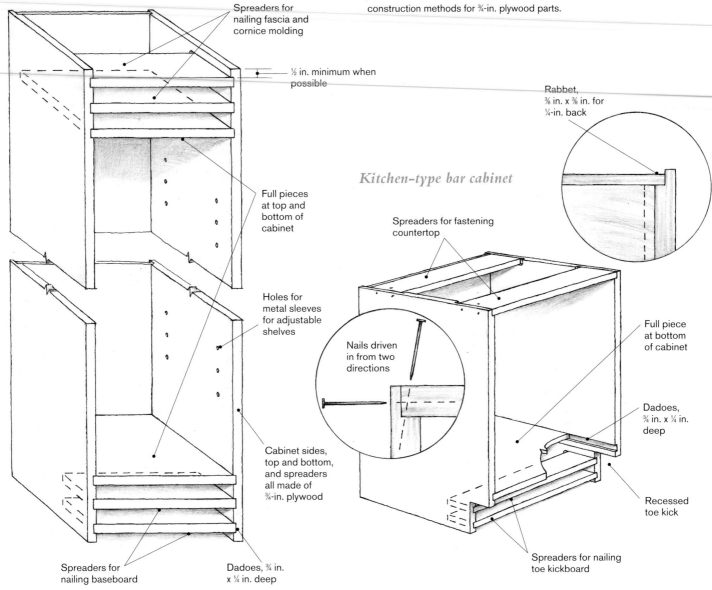

Spreaders for nailing fascia and cornice molding

½ in. minimum when possible

Rabbet, ⅜ in. x ⅜ in. for ¼-in. back

Full pieces at top and bottom of cabinet

Holes for metal sleeves for adjustable shelves

Spreaders for fastening countertop

Full piece at bottom of cabinet

Nails driven in from two directions

Dadoes, ¾ in. x ¼ in. deep

Cabinet sides, top and bottom, and spreaders all made of ¾-in. plywood

Recessed toe kick

Spreaders for nailing baseboard

Dadoes, ¾ in. x ¼ in. deep

Spreaders for nailing toe kickboard

Pre-Finish Case Work Before Assembly

Except for the occasional odd box, we usually apply finishes before putting the cases together. The finishing process goes faster and we get better results, without any overspray buildup in the corners. With the cabinets for this library, we applied a pigment-based oil stain, sealed and sanded that, then topcoated all the cabinet parts with two coats of nitrocellulose lacquer. (We usually don't bother to apply masking tape to the joints, unless the glue joint is an important structural factor. That would be the case with a cabinet that will be hung on a wall and loaded with a lot of weight.) On-site, once all the cabinets are installed, we finish up with a coat of Butcher's wax.

When we put boxes together, we most often use glue and nails, through-nailed from the side of all the rabbets and dadoes and toenailed on an angle from the top and bottom of the rabbets (see the drawing on p. 15). The nails mechanically reinforce the glue joint and keep the pieces from pulling apart under the stress of handling when cabinets are delivered and installed.

I'm partial to coated nails. We use 5-penny resin-coated box nails. The diameter is only a little larger than a 4-penny, but the length is almost that of a 6-penny nail. The nails penetrate deeply, and the shank does not split the plywood. Coated nails hold better than any gun-driven nail of the same length, and I can always stop hammering when a nail starts to come out the other side of the cabinet piece. It doesn't take much longer to put the boxes together this way, and it's worth it.

With some case work, especially if there are many parts that have to go together at the same time, we use screws instead of nails and glue. An example would be a case with a lot of drawers that has dust board dividers between each drawer. For that, we use No. 6 trim-head screws with a square-head drive. When spreaders are spaced every 6 in. or so along the full height of the cabinet, there will be plenty of fasteners and glue isn't really necessary.

In most cases, if your plywood pieces and their edges have all been cut square, then the box goes together square. (That's another reason why I like a full-width rabbet; it gives you a full surface on the bottom of the rabbet as a square surface to draw the two pieces together.) When we finish assembling a box, we check it for square. If there's any problem, and there rarely is one, we true it up with clamps before the glue sets in the joints.

JOHN WEST operates Cope and Mould Millwork, Inc., in Danbury, Connecticut.

INSTALLING THE CASE WORK.
Job-site conditions usually require shims to make cases level and plumb. The result is a beautiful library and plenty of sawdust back at the shop

Cabinets Built for the Long Haul

BY BILL CROZIER

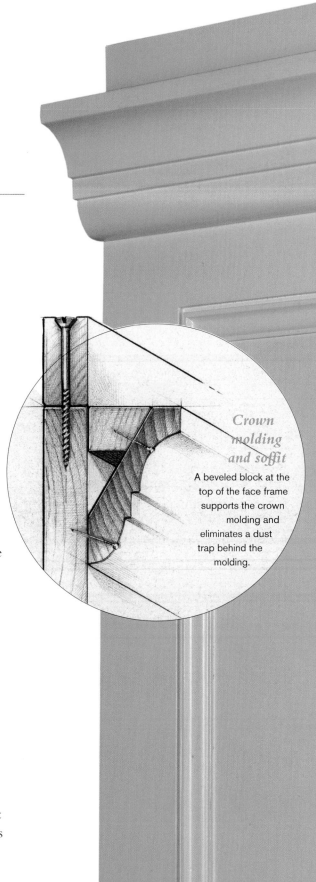

Crown molding and soffit

A beveled block at the top of the face frame supports the crown molding and eliminates a dust trap behind the molding.

CAULING ALL CLAMPS. Strips of wood, called cauls, are placed between the clamps and the face frame to prevent marring. The author uses numerous clamps when gluing the face frame to the cabinet's plywood carcase.

For the past several years I have had a lot of clients in New York City, about 175 miles away from my cabinet shop in Providence, R.I. When I finish the cabinets in the shop, everything gets packed in my truck, and I head down Interstate 95, one of the most heavily traveled roads in the country. Some of the roadway bumps are more like jumps, and some of the potholes are more like sinkholes. It's a jarring ride, and if you're not going 65 mph, you're in danger of getting run off the road by everyone else who's going even faster.

Typically, the cabinets I build require the fitting and hanging of numerous doors and drawers. And as anybody who has hung even one door or drawer knows, precision in the execution is of the utmost importance, especially if the job is going to be made to last for a long time, to continue to work properly, and to survive the trip to the big city.

I construct cabinetwork in such a way that the final product meets many criteria. The cabinet must be incredibly strong, be very, very square, and take lots of abuse without showing signs of wear over a long period of time. The last and most important criterion is that the construction techniques be based around machinery that I have in

Molded stiles and rails for glazed doors

Long, 1½-in. by ⁵⁄₁₆-in. tenons provide more gluing surface than a standard coped joint with a stub tenon.

French Lap joint on doors

A beaded half-lap joint, called a French lap, adds a decorative touch to upper and lower cabinet doors.

the shop. Most of the systems I use are very low tech.

Increasingly, it seems, many woodworkers think that if they get bigger, more expensive machines, the productivity and ease of construction will improve. Sometimes this is the case, but anyone with a small core of simple machinery can construct cabinets of superior strength and durability quite easily.

Good Materials Make a Good Cabinet

Lots of time spent building a cabinet can be wasted by using anything but the best materials available, in the selection of both solid wood and sheet goods as well as in the choice of hardware.

A lot of the cabinets I build get painted. To some, the term "paint grade" implies that the materials and the construction techniques used can be less than the best because everything gets covered by coats of paint. Aside from the fact that I use medium-density fiberboard (MDF), which is more stable than solid wood, for the door and end panels, the only difference between a painted cabinet and an unpainted cabinet is the paint. And in fact, the design of a painted cabinet may be more important than that of an unpainted one. In a painted, monochromatic cabinet, one's eye is not taken in and possibly swayed by beautifully finished hardwood; rather, one sees the clean lines and sculptural beauty of the cabinet's design.

All plywood is not the same I build all of my cabinets with ¾-in.-thick plywood for the sides, bottoms, and tops. I use veneer-core plywood of the best possible grade with a face veneer of either maple or birch. And because veneer glue seams can show through a painted surface (on the interior of clear-coated cabinets—varnished, lacquered, or polyurethaned—you'll see a continuous veneer seam), I always specify that at least one side of the plywood be a

AN ANCIENT MACHINE IN A LOW-TECH SHOP. The author uses a 60-year-old single-end tenoning machine to mill cabinet parts. Aside from this machine, his shop is decidedly low tech. Good materials, solid joinery, and quality hardware make his cabinets bulletproof.

WPF, or "whole piece face veneer." This means that there are no glue seams in the veneer on the good side of the sheet. Random glue seams can lead to a somewhat haphazard appearance.

I use ½-in.-thick maple or birch WPF veneer-core plywood for cabinet backs. A ½-in.-thick cabinet back is far superior to the ¼-in.-thick industry-standard back. It adds structural integrity to the cabinet and doesn't sound hollow if you bang it. Lots of cabinets with ¼-in.-thick backs are mounted to the wall through ¾-in. wood cleats screwed across the backs of the cabinets. The cleats dictate where the cabinets can be screwed to the wall, and they break up the clean lines inside the cabinet.

All pieces of a cabinet carcase are dadoed for alignment and glued and screwed together. I run a ½-in. dado around the perimeter of the carcase's back to accommodate the ½-in.-thick plywood back. The back is then screwed and glued directly onto the rear of the cabinet. This creates a strong, square, bulletproof plywood box.

For painted kitchen cabinets, I build all of my drawers using ⅝-in.-thick Baltic birch plywood for the sides and ½-in. plywood for the bottoms. The multiple veneers of the Baltic birch, free of voids, look sharp as drawer components. I clear coat all drawers with a conversion varnish.

For the lower door and end panels of my cabinets, I use ½-in. MDF, rabbeted to fit into the ⁵⁄₁₆-in. dadoes in the stiles and rails.

Buy 5/4 Soft Maple for Face Frames and Doors

A well-constructed face frame will give the front of a cabinet strength and durability, and all of the pieces will stay smooth and flush. A poorly assembled face frame will result in joinery that does not remain flush, and it can look shabby very quickly; remember, the wood is constantly moving.

I buy 5/4 soft maple for all face-frame and door parts. Soft maple is not only more stable than poplar, but it also is considerably harder, takes paint exceptionally well, and is only slightly more costly. I have also noticed over the years that when I try to paint over the dark portions of poplar—those black and purple streaks that occasionally appear—it takes more than two finish coats of paint to cover them. Soft maple has a consistent off-white color.

Typically when I start a job, the first thing I do is rough-mill the face-frame, door, and drawer-front stock to 1⅛ in. thick, sticker it, and let it sit. Then I go about my business of constructing the plywood portions of the cabinets, which, depending on the size of the job, can last from one to six weeks. During this time, the solid stock can sit around, twist, move, or do whatever it is going to do before I finish milling it.

I make all of my face frames and drawer fronts a full 1 in. thick. The stiles and rails for the doors are milled to ¹⁵⁄₁₆ in. thick. The difference in thickness between the face frame and doors allows me to use unobtrusive ¹⁄₁₆-in.-thick vinyl door bumpers for the flush-mount doors.

A 1-in.-thick face frame is much more stable than the industry's standard ¾-in.-thick frame, and the extra thickness allows for stronger joinery possibilities and more options for different molding thicknesses on the doors and end panels. Plus, it looks better; you immediately see that it is stout.

I use full mortise-and-tenon joints on my face frames. To make the mortises, I use a Multico hollow chisel mortiser, which is a fairly inexpensive machine to purchase new, and it is really fantastic. I tenon all of my pieces using a ca. 1935 Fay and Egan Lightning 505 single-end tenoning machine, but tenons are also easily made with a tenoning jig on the table saw. All mortises are 1⅜ in. deep, and the tenons are 1¼ in. long. I haunch all face-frame tenons so that the surface of the face frame remains flat and smooth over time.

After a dry assembly, the face frame is glued together. I take the utmost care to glue it up square. The openings in the face frame are where all of the doors and drawers are to be hung. If things are not parallel and square, the job of hanging doors and drawer fronts will soon become frustrating and difficult.

After the face frame has been glued together, the front and back are handplaned, scraped, and sanded smooth. Then I glue the frame onto the front of the plywood carcase, using either nails or biscuits for alignment. I place the carcase on its back on sawhorses and use every clamp I own for

A well-constructed face frame will give the front of a cabinet strength and durability, and all of the pieces will stay smooth and flush.

Bulletproof Cabinets

There are no shortcuts in these cabinets. The author admits that his materials cost a little more and his techniques take a little longer than the industry standards. Inch-thick face frames and doors, full mortise-and-tenon joinery, and quality hardware are some of the hallmarks of his cabinetry.

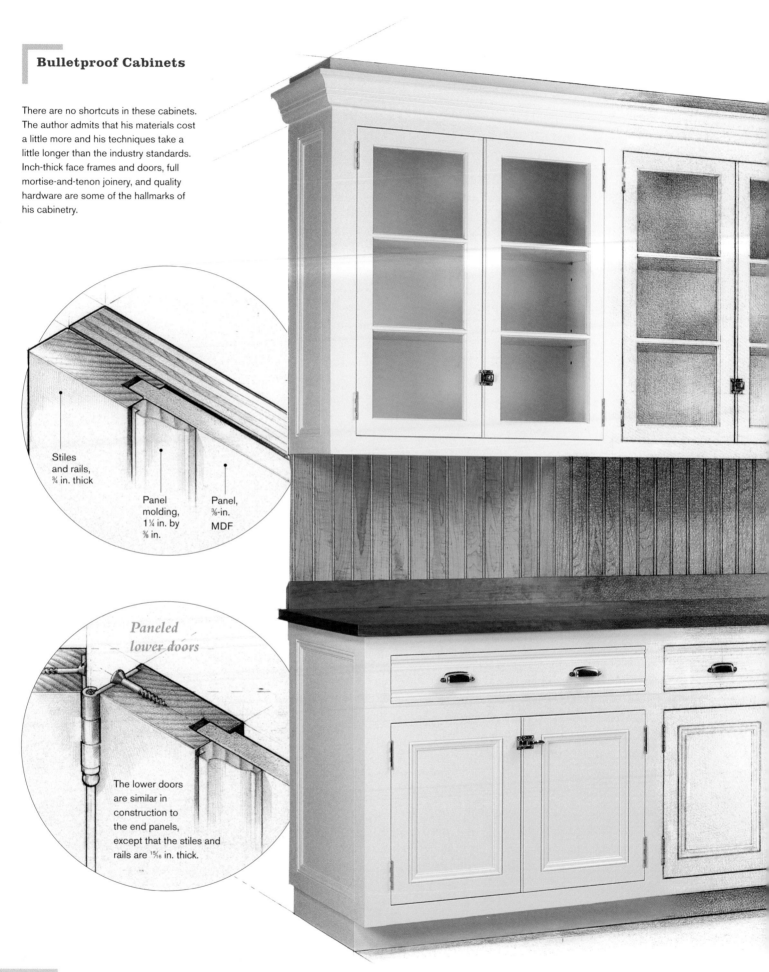

Stiles and rails, ¾ in. thick

Panel molding, 1¼ in. by ⅜ in.

Panel, ⅜-in. MDF

Paneled lower doors

The lower doors are similar in construction to the end panels, except that the stiles and rails are 1⁵⁄₁₆ in. thick.

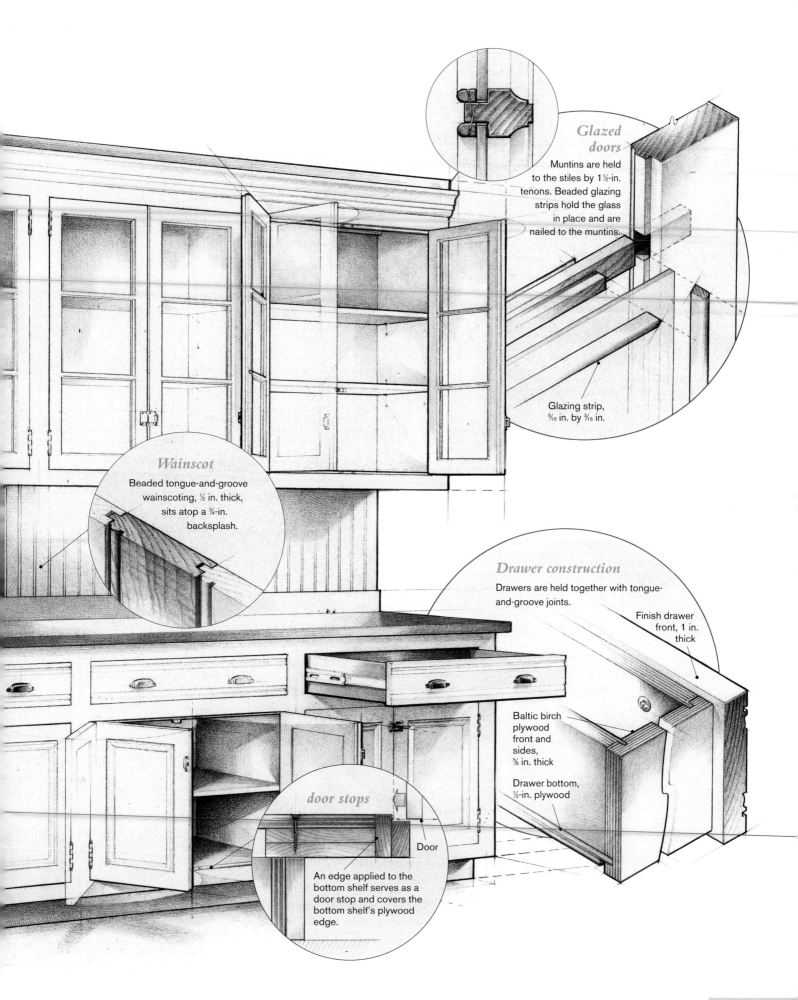

Glazed doors

Muntins are held to the stiles by 1½-in. tenons. Beaded glazing strips hold the glass in place and are nailed to the muntins.

Glazing strip, ⁵⁄₁₆ in. by ³⁄₁₆ in.

Wainscot

Beaded tongue-and-groove wainscoting, ½ in. thick, sits atop a ¾-in. backsplash.

Drawer construction

Drawers are held together with tongue-and-groove joints.

Finish drawer front, 1 in. thick

Baltic birch plywood front and sides, ⅝ in. thick

Drawer bottom, ½-in. plywood

door stops

An edge applied to the bottom shelf serves as a door stop and covers the bottom shelf's plywood edge.

Door

the glue-up. Remember, the edge of a piece of veneer-core plywood has only 50% glue surface because half of the veneered core is end grain and will not accept glue. So a really good glue-up with lots of clamps and even pressure everywhere is of the utmost importance.

SIMILAR DESIGNS, DIFFERENT APPLICATIONS.
The author builds lots of cabinetry for turn-of-the century New York City apartments. Shelves in glazed upper cabinets line up with door muntins.

The glazed upper doors and paneled lower doors are built with mortise and tenons. And I make my drawers as five-sided boxes, adding a separate, full-inch drawer front to cover the ends of the slides.

Quality Hardware is a Good Investment

Adjustable cup hinges have been popular in kitchens for the past couple of decades. Sure, they're easy to install, and you can adjust them every which way, including loose, and that's my problem with the things. The doors look great when they leave the shop, but inevitably the hinges go out of whack. Subsequently, every cup-hinged kitchen I've seen has doors as crooked as a witch's teeth.

I hang all of my cabinet doors on high-quality, removable-pin butt hinges. I buy top-quality Baldwin®, Vin-Morris, Merit®, Ball and Ball®, Brusso® or Whitechapel® hinges. The hinge knuckles are machined and not rolled, so there is no play in the swinging action of a door. I usually use a Stanley® roller catch and vinyl bumpers that soften the closing of the door. Spend the time hanging the door correctly, and it will stay that way forever.

Don't skimp on drawer slides; for a few dollars more per pair, you get an infinitely better product. I have used epoxy-painted Accuride® slides for years and find them well made and easy to install.

Granted, the materials and procedures laid out here may cost slightly more and take a bit more time to complete, but in the end, building a better mousetrap is what it is all about. To make products more affordable, many manufacturers use cheaper materials and take shortcuts to make the company more profitable. I believe that the better-built product will prevail.

BILL CROZIER builds his cabinets in Providence, Rhode Island.

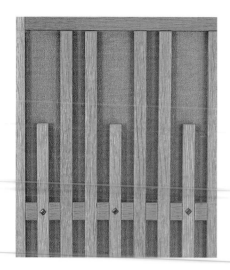

Extraordinary Built-Ins

BY ROSS DAY

A few years ago, two women walked into my shop unannounced. One of them was the daughter of a client; the other was her interior designer. They were familiar with my furniture and asked whether I would consider making built-in cabinets for them. I said I was not doing cabinets anymore, just furniture. But the women said they didn't want cabinets in the traditional sense. They were looking for built-ins that looked like high-quality furniture.

My curiosity was piqued, because I had never done anything like this before. Case-good construction and furniture making really are two separate disciplines. Built-in cabinets generally are utilitarian in nature. To keep costs under control, the choice of materials and construction follow certain predictable paths. For one, doors often are attached with large European-style hinges, and drawers are usually set on metal slides, all of which make for easier adjustment and faster construction. Cabinets usually are

BY COMBINING HIS FURNITURE-MAKING SENSIBILITIES with good case construction techniques, the author designed and built this bedroom furniture that looks like high-quality built-ins.

Taking Case Goods
to a New Level

Although technically still a built-in, "cabineture" has its feet planted firmly in the traditions of fine furniture. Standard-quality cabinets lack the refinements of "cabineture."

Commercially veneered plywood or particleboard case is screwed, doweled, or biscuited together.

Typical cabinet

Visible nail rail inside cabinet

Stub tenons

Thin, iron-on edge-banding

Euro-style cup hinges

Veneered or solid-wood raised panel

"Cabineture"

Nail rail is hidden behind valance.

Solid wood valance

Doors are assembled using bridle joints.

Biscuit joints, 6 in. o.c.

Handmade pulls

Custom-veneered MDF case

Veneered panel

Applied latticework or other custom detail

Dowels at front corners of carcase add strength.

Butt hinges

Solid-wood edge-banding (⅛ in. thick)

attached to walls with screws, and moldings, if any, are nailed in place.

Fine furniture requires more handwork, such as hand-cut dovetail joints, which are time-consuming and costly if done on a large scale. But furniture presents the builder (and client) with many more options. The choices of materials are endless and the design possibilities vast. These are all the reasons why I got into furniture making and why I took on this commission.

Designing a Bedroom from Scratch

My mission was to create a refuge—a place to relax, reflect, and re-energize. The homeowners are both avid readers and art collectors and demanded lots of storage and display space. Their wish list included an entertainment/display center, a corner cabinet, three sliding door screens, three large wardrobes, two bookcases, and even some freestanding furniture: a platform bed and two nightstands. Aesthetically, the clients were after what they called a "contemporary Asian feeling."

I looked for a traditional and historical link that I could update and found it in a book on Japanese architecture. I was intrigued by a style of fence and gate that utilized a latticework pattern with decorative nails at the joints. I sketched out various ideas and came up with a scaled-down version of this latticework pattern, which could be repeated throughout the room. The clients liked the idea. The latticework, which is applied to all of the door panels, became the focal point of many of the pieces, both large and small, and helped tie them all together visually.

Top-Quality Materials Make a Difference

The clients requested that the primary wood be Japanese oak, a tight-grained, honey-colored wood. Unfortunately, it isn't available anymore. I was, however, able to track down some old-growth quartersawn American white oak and quartersawn French oak veneer. These are lighter in color and finer in grain than typical white oak and turned out to be a good match.

All of the boxes and panels were veneered medium-density fiberboard (MDF). Edges were covered with solid, shopmade banding, about ⅛ in. thick. Thicker edge-banding allowed me to ease the corners and provided a durable surface. I also used solid maple, primarily for drawer sides and backs. To keep shelves from sagging, I first built up a core of a ¾-in. plywood surfaced on both sides with ¼-in. MDF. Then I veneered the faces and finished off the shelves with ¾-in.-thick edge-banding.

The designer provided handmade pulls from India. But when I first saw them, I wasn't too thrilled. The pulls were coated with layers of lacquer, shielding highly polished brass. To soften the glare, I sandblasted the pulls and other hardware and chemically treated them to yield a more subtle, antique brown finish.

The designer also suggested using some fabrics as an accent. The door panels of the entertainment center were wrapped in silk, and the corner cabinet was adorned with straw matting. These fabrics added color and texture to the overall scheme.

Joinery Ranged from Biscuits to Hand-cut Dovetails

I used exposed joinery throughout. All of the rails and stiles were connected with bridle joints (also known as slip joints). The tops of lower cabinets (and nightstands) were veneered and framed with solid

wood, then joined at the corner with bridle
joints. The rails and stiles of the headboard
were joined the same way.

All drawers have variable-spaced hand-
cut dovetails with narrow pins. The drawers
were built upon frames (called NK drawers)
that act as slides, in tandem with wooden
guides. NK drawers are very strong, and because the drawer sides don't contact the
case, drawers are easy to open and close.

The boxes themselves were fashioned
like typical built-ins. Biscuits were used to
join the cases, and the backs were glued into rabbets. But biscuits don't have a lot of
holding power at the narrow ends. So I
added dowel joints at the front corners of
the cases to make sure they would stay
tight. Side-by-side cases were connected to
each other using joint-connector bolts,
which I tinted antique brown to match the
rest of the hardware.

CARCASE CONSTRUCTION IS PRETTY
STRAIGHTFORWARD. But lots of work
went into the doors. Bridle joints are used
on all of the rails and stiles. On the inside,
sliding wire racks are used for storage.

HAND-CUT JOINTS AND HANDMADE PULLS FROM INDIA. All of the drawers have variably spaced, hand-cut dovetails. The author sandblasted the shiny original finish on the pulls, then patinated them antique brown.

Time Spent Refining Details Pays Off

The word details implies small or subordinate, but in furniture, details are as important as the materials, joinery, and overall design. Screw up the details, and the entire project is weaker as a result. Take shadow lines, for example. If a cabinet has too few, it looks bland; too many, and it takes on a busy look. On traditional doors, shadow lines typically are achieved through the use of raised panels and profiled rails and stiles. This project had none of those details; instead, I created shadow lines by varying the thickness of parts. For example, the rails are $\frac{3}{32}$ in. thinner than the stiles on all of the doors. The latticework on the flat panels is set back from the rails by another $\frac{3}{32}$ in. The valances that run atop all of the pieces are gapped, leaving a ¼-in. shadow line. Addi-

tionally, the bridle joints on the corners of the headboard, nightstand top, and a few other places are emphasized. Either the tenon is proud or the walls of the mortise protrude by a small amount.

The exposed-joinery concept was carried over to the latticework. Where members cross, I added diamond-shaped brass pins, which were patinated to match the rest of the hardware.

A New Discipline Is Born

When it came time to deliver and install the cabinets, I remembered one of the reasons why I got out of cabinetmaking. This can be tough, dangerous work. It took three guys and a Genie® Lift to get everything in place. We had to build a bridge over a sunken living room to make a platform big enough to get the lift in position. Then the cabinets took a slow, wobbly ride up 12 ft. before being pulled over the railing to the second floor. That each box made it safely into the room was a minor miracle.

All built-ins must be fitted to walls, which are never perfectly plumb nor flat. To fit these cabinets, I used scribe strips. The cabinets were held back approximately ¾ in. from the walls, and the strips were hand-planed to fill the gap. The method made fitting a lot easier and added another shadow line to the rather plain sides of the bookshelves and wardrobes.

This job would have been a lot harder to accomplish had I not been trained in both basic cabinetry and furniture making. For this challenging project, I drew on all of my skills, and that led me to a new standard of woodworking, somewhere in the great divide between case goods and fine furniture. I call this hybrid "cabineture," a style of working that combines the craftsmanship and ideals of both disciplines.

ROSS DAY builds custom furniture in Poulsbo, Washington, and teaches furniture making part-time at the community-college level.

FABRIC ADDS TEXTURE. The top of the corner cabinet is covered in straw matting. The same material is also applied to the soffit.

A Woodworker's Guide to Medium-Density Fiberboard

BY JIM HAYDEN

Medium-density fiberboard, or MDF as it is more commonly known, is the newest of the furniture-quality wood composites. Because of its dense, uniform composition and flatness, it has surpassed plywood and particleboard as the sheet good of choice for fine work and more routine uses.

Pre-finished faces are flat as the slate on a pool table, which along with its dimensional stability makes it an excellent substrate for veneer. The edges machine well, with no chipout, and MDF accepts a full range of joinery and fasteners.

But if you have never seen a 4x8 or 5x8 sheet of MDF or have never even heard of MDF, you have plenty of company. MDF has been an industrial product for its entire 28-year history, with most shipments earmarked for furniture factories and cabinet producers. Only recently has it become more available to retail consumers and small shops. Once you have some MDF in your shop, you may find, as I have, that it is also good stuff to make some of your jigs, fixtures, and templates.

Whether you use it for jigs or the substrate for fine veneered furniture, there are some special tricks and tips for using MDF. I'll share what I've learned from my own experience and from research done for the National Particleboard Association℠ (NPA), which includes eight of the nine MDF companies, as well as from the reactions of woodworkers who regularly use MDF in the cabinet shop of the Arthur M. Sackler and Freer Galleries in the Smithsonian Institution (see the photos on p. 34).

Machining MDF

Because it's homogeneous (see the inset photo on the facing page), MDF machines better than plywood or particleboard and even some natural woods. There are no layers or chips, brittle edges, knots, or grain. I routed all 15 types of MDF made in the United States, courtesy of the nine MDF companies (see the photo on the facing page). The boards share a sameness in meeting industry standards: They match in density and superb flatness. They differ because the trees harvested near the plants differ. The wood chips, shavings, and sawdust (or residuals) from the local sawmills and plywood mills are the raw material of MDF. Also, the companies use proprietary formulas, thus adding a few minor, and in some cases, a few major differences, such as formaldehyde content.

A VARIETY OF DIFFERENT TYPES OF MEDIUM-DENSITY FIBERBOARD **(MDF) are available from nine companies that manufacture the material. Although it has been used in industry for 28 years, MDF is just now becoming more available to consumers and small shops. The difference in density is obvious when comparing MDF, left side, to common particleboard, right side.**

I've used two brands of MDF regularly during the last five years. I'm impressed with the consistently smooth surface of the sheets. MDF starts out as a low-density, 15-in.-thick slab 18 ft. long. A ¾-in. board is compressed at 800 lb. pressure, then 50,000 lb. pressure to almost final thickness. Sanders, in a series of grits, take over and finish off with 120 or 150 grit, sanding and burnishing to precisely ¾ in.

Sometimes I measure new sheets. I find their thickness to be scrupulously maintained. However, extreme heat and humidity changes, such as daily changes encountered with outdoor storage, will cause a permanent thickness increase. But the thicker boards, ¾ in. and 1 in., will take some abuse in storage (i.e., stored on edge) and not warp.

Sawing A 50-tooth combination blade is suggested for rough-cutting large sections of MDF on the table saw. But I make so many things out of cutoff pieces that I go right to my finish-cut blade. That used to be a 60-tooth triple-chip. I loved that blade; with a pair of hold-downs and my pride and joy, a shopmade, European-style adjustable splitter, a piece of MDF would

The edges machine well, with no chipout, and MDF accepts a full range of joinery and fasteners.

MUSEUM-QUALITY MDF. **These display cases at the Freer Gallery of the Smithsonian Institution show off some of MDF's versatility. The case pictured above shows the crisp edge-holding ability of MDF in a painted piece. The case shown below makes use of walnut-veneered MDF with solid-wood moldings.**

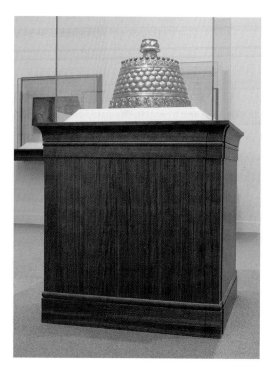

slide down the fence and exit the blade with a new edge so smooth that I had to stroke it. Then I bought the other blade manufacturers recommended for MDF, a 60-tooth thin-kerf alternate top bevel (mine is a Freud TFLU88). It seemed to cut even cleaner than the triple-chip, and material moved more easily through the blade because of its semi-thin kerf (nominally 0.090 in.). Its teeth angles fit the NPA's specs for a blade to saw cleanly top and bottom surfaces of overlaid panels. They are a 15° hook, 15° top bevel, and a 10° alternate face bevel.

I use 6-in. blade stiffeners for a slightly finer cut, and I made a zero-clearance insert to keep the dust down where it belongs. I'll talk more about MDF dust problems and solutions later.

My friends in the cabinet shop have good results using the table saw to kerf MDF sheets, so they can be bent into curved forms.

Edge-shaping and routing When I saw or rout an edge, rabbet, or dado for joining, I get sharp edges with MDF. The edge surface looks and feels smooth. When rubbed counter to the cut direction, it feels slightly fuzzy or scratchy, depending on the brand of MDF, but the piece is ready for glue-up and assembly. My contoured router cuts (cove, roundover, and Roman ogee) are clean and smooth, with crisp edge profiles. The edge surface is a little rougher than on straight cuts, but that disappears with normal light sanding for finishing. When routing or shaping, feed MDF about 25% slower than wood for maximum edge smoothness.

MDF does have its limits. Sharp protruding contoured edges aren't a good choice. And being 10% urea-formaldehyde or other glue, MDF does wear down cutters faster than wood.

MDF sawdust is fine resin-coated particles of wood dust, light enough to become airborne and settle on everything in sight. Building a router table/table saw extension with vacuum attachments has virtually eliminated floating dust and cut down on my set-up time (see the photo at left on p. 36). I use a high-quality dust mask, the Dustfoe® 66, which I purchased from Highland Hardware and have installed vacuum setups on all my machine tools.

I wanted the same low-dust environment for freehand routing, so I built an acrylic and MDF safety guard/vacuum hookup that bolts into T-nuts epoxied on the underside of my router base plate. It is almost 100% effective with MDF dust.

KERFS FOR A CURVE. Woodworkers at the Sackler Gallery cabinet shop in the Smithsonian Institution kerf-bend veneered MDF to make a curved museum bench.

CRISP PROFILES. Medium-density fiberboard excels in maintaining sharp edge profiles. Shown here are, from left, examples of cove, roundover, and Roman ogee, all created with a router.

Successful sanding Other advice to the contrary, don't sand an MDF panel before attaching an overlay. Scuff-sanding can cause a weaker glue bond. I just make sure my work table and the panel faces are nice and clean, then proceed.

Flat and contoured edges should be sanded before finishing to remove the nap. A belt sander is a good choice for flat

SHOP-BUILT ATTACHMENTS HANDLE MDF'S DUST on the author's router table. Built as an extension of his table-saw table, the router table houses a shop vacuum and sound baffling, which makes for quiet, dust-free operation.

DEALING WITH DUST. A worker in the Sackler Gallery cabinet shop at the Smithsonian Institution avoids the fine dust produced by MDF by wearing a Racal powered respirator while finish-sanding a display cabinet.

edges, as is an abrasive wheel for contoured edges. Use a sequence of 100 to 150 grit, or 120 to 180 grit. It's a light sanding, not a dust raiser. Some shops prefer hand-sanding.

Sanding also is the process that can raise the most of MDF's extra-fine dust. At our cabinet shop in the Smithsonian, the helmet-type powered air-purifying respirator is used (see the photo at right).

Joinery and Glue Choices

MDF machines and glues well, giving it literally a sharp edge over plywood and particleboard in joint-making. "We do a lot of case work with Medex MDF, using miter joints," explains a cabinetmaker at the Smithsonian. "I have to be careful handling the Medex edges. They are so sharp I've cut my fingers several times."

The furniture and cabinet industries use dowels extensively in MDF case work. Drawers are often made with 7/16-in. dovetailed or rabbeted MDF sides. Independent furniture and cabinetmakers seem to be sold on biscuit joinery for MDF. If you use dowels, spiral and grooved dowels are recommended over plain dowels by eight of the nine MDF companies.

The joints that work well with MDF (as shown in the photo on the facing page) include: loose tenons (spline tenons), dovetails, sliding dovetails, and finger joints. Spline or biscuit miters, lock miters, miter and rabbet joints, simple miters, rabbets, dadoes, and butt joints with biscuits or dowels also work well.

Adhesives A high solids or gap-filling glue is ideal for MDF. I use modified (yellow) polyvinyl acetate (PVA) or Titebond II when assembly time permits. Otherwise, it's white PVA, the same as I'd use for wood. Contact cement, epoxy, and urea resin work well when needed. A factory method is to use a hot-pressed rigid resin to bond an MDF core and hardwood veneer. Under low pressure at 250° for less than three minutes, the thermosetting glue doubles the panel's stiffness. I would rate urea resin and epoxy as the best thermosetting glue candidates, but it's best to make your own tests on scrap for any setup before the final glue-up.

Hardware and Fasteners

A straight-shanked screw with deep, wide, sharp threads is best for MDF. I use Robertson® square drive, particleboard, and sheet-metal screws. (On the West Coast, a savvy MDF user recommends Twinfast® particleboard screws.) The fine-threaded sheet metal or self-tapping screw is also good. And drywall screws make handy temporary holders for MDF projects.

Do not use tapered wood screws. Screw threads cut MDF fibers and resins. While regular wood springs back, MDF distorts. The distortion and tapered screw shape combine to make for poor fastening.

There's a limit to the screw size an edge will take without splitting (see the chart on p. 38). Use longer (not larger) screws in the edge for increased strength. More screws add strength, up to 4 in. apart.

Drill pilot holes in the edge, so the board won't split, and drill them to the depth the screw will be inserted, plus about ¼ in. It's also a good idea to drill pilot holes in the face plane. See the chart for common screw sizes and correct pilot holes.

Screws in the face should be at least 1 in. away from corners, and edge screws should be 3 in. from corners. A slow drill speed or dull bit will burnish the pilot hole wall and cause crumbling. Run a sharp bit at high speed (3,000 rpm for industrial applications). You'll get a clean, accurate hole with top pull strength.

There's a "turns" trick to make sure you don't over-torque and strip the panel threads. A three-quarter turn past flush on

A WIDE VARIETY OF JOINERY is possible with MDF. Examples shown here surrounding a routed dovetail joint are, clockwise from left, biscuits, dado, rabbet and dado, spline miter, and biscuited miter. The background is a sheet of factory-veneered MDF.

USING SCREWS IN MDF

Screw size	Pilot hole	Minimum edge*
#6	$\frac{3}{32}$ in.	$\frac{1}{2}$ in.
#8	$\frac{7}{64}$ in.	$\frac{5}{8}$ in.
#10	$\frac{1}{8}$ in.	1 in.

*Minimum sheet thickness for driving screws into an edge without splitting.

the face is maximum torque. A three-eighths turn past flush on the edge is the limit there. Even with a properly sized and countersunk pilot hole, the screw will break away beyond these points.

My friends in the cabinet shop sometimes use pneumatically driven ring-shank coated nails or coated staples on glued joints to save clamping time. If you do that, be careful not to drive edge staples with their legs parallel to the surface, or you may get splitting.

Hinges After trying all sorts of hinges, I found the best hinges for MDF attach face to face. When hinges are installed, MDF may "pyramid," or develop a bump around hinge screws. To prevent the pyramid and to ensure the hinge is flush, drill a partial countersink along with the pilot holes.

Laminating, Veneering, and Finishing

Good bonding strength, dimensional stability, flatness, and other qualities previously mentioned make MDF an ideal substrate for numerous materials, including high-pressure laminates and veneers. Cross-banding is unnecessary with even the thinnest veneers.

Either veneers or paint can be used to finish edges. A painted edge may work well with laminated, veneered, or, of course, painted face planes. It involves a typical edge-finishing process. Careful sanding is followed by one or two coats of sealer. Burnish smooth each coat of sealer before applying the final topcoat.

Quick-drying sanding sealers, auto-body primers, and even white PVA glues diluted 20% can be used as edge sealers.

Sealing in formaldehyde may be a factor in finish selection. The level of formaldehyde in untreated MDF may remain above ambient levels for several years.

High-pressure laminates offer almost total sealing, matching factory-applied thin and thick vinyls. After that comes alkyd oil primer and oil enamel paint combined, two coats of polyurethane, and latex-ammonia combined with two coats of latex wall paint. (The latex-ammonia types will raise the grain.) Ironically, the effective alkyd oil finishes contain formaldehyde, but it normally off-gases in two weeks.

Finishes that are less effective sealers include: oil based or lacquer sealer plus a top coat of varnish or lacquer; two coats of lacquer or oil primer; lacquer sanding sealer plus one or two coats clear lacquer; quick-drying lacquer sanding sealers; and shellac or varnish applied without a sealer.

Despite their other merits, finishes that will not effectively seal in formaldehyde in MDF include: two coats of regular latex paint, penetrating oil sealer, stains, waxes, or linseed oil.

There are treated low-formaldehyde MDFs, such as Plum Creek®, and formaldehyde-free brands, such as Medite II and Medex (exterior grade), to consider. I asked the Sackler and Freer cabinet shop supervisor, Cornell Evans, for his impressions of Medex. "Medex has no formaldehyde and is fire-rated. It is lighter and harder than (regular) MDF," he said. "It glues better and takes paint better. We use it for case work. It has sharp edges, is water repellent, and is much less dusty (than other MDFs). There is no fine sawdust when cutting. We use $\frac{5}{8}$-in. Medex in place of $\frac{3}{4}$-in. MDF."

Finding and Buying MDF

Standard MDF costs about 60% less than seven-ply birch plywood and about 40% more than particleboard. And formaldehyde-free, water-resistant Medex-type MDF is about triple the cost of particleboard, but it is still 15% less than top-quality birch plywood.

Locating and buying medium-density fiberboard is sometimes difficult because so much of it goes directly to industry. In the summer of 1990, several MDF companies began test-marketing their products around the country.

California is a big test market. The Medite Corporation based in Medford, Ore., is placing ¾-in. Medite® in 20 home improvement stores there. J.E. Higgins, a chain of small lumberyards, has MDF in their yards in Los Angeles, San Francisco, and Sacramento.

Some chains have MDF in selected stores across the country. The stores include Handy Dandy and Lowes. Sequoia Supply in Columbia, Md., distributes Plum Creek MDF to lumberyards in parts of Maryland, Virginia, and Pennsylvania.

If you know of mills that cater to wood-workers, call them. If you must special order, local independent dealers are your best bet. A chain that has particleboard but no MDF may be able to order some for you from its particleboard source, but you will pay top dollar.

Small commercial shops can buy from one of the 2,000 industrial wood products distributors in the United States. Would the industrial distributor welcome me if I showed up as an individual to buy one or two sheets? Probably not. But my 275-member Washington Woodworkers Guild has an agreement with one to sell to all our members, large orders or small. (Guilds have buying power. We have price discounts from several stores, wholesalers, and manufacturers.) Don't overlook the fact that some sellers are willing to deliver sheet material.

If all else fails, write one or more of the MDF companies listed below, and tell them everything you went through and how badly you want their product. If you have equally interested friends or belong to a guild with a genuine interest in MDF among its members, mention that also. No one is promising you instant results, but many letters from many woodworkers do a market make.

JIM HAYDEN is an amateur woodworker and a professional photographer at the Arthur M. Sackler Gallery and Freer Gallery in the Smithsonian Institution, Washington, D.C.

Sources

Georgia-Pacific Corp., Holly Hill
133 Peachtree St., N.E.
PO Box 105605
Atlanta, GA 30348
www.gp.com

International Paper
Masonite Division
Spring Hope Plant
Highway 64
PO Box 369
Spring Hope, NC 27882
www.internationalpaper.com

Louisiana-Pacific Corp.
Eufaula Mill
Route 3, Box 22
Clayton, AL 36016
www.lpcorp.com

Medite Division of SierraPine Ltd.
2151 Professional Drive, Suite 200
Roseville CA 95661
800-676-3339
www.sierrapine.com

Norbord Industries, Inc.
PO Box 26
Deposit, NY 13754
www.norbord.com

Plum Creek Manufacturing, L.P.
PO Box 160
Columbia Falls, MT 59912
www.plumcreek.com

Weyerhaeuser Co.
PO Box 290
Moncure, NC 27559
www.weyerhaeuser.com

Working with Synthetic Countertop Materials

BY KEN PICOU

Synthetic countertop materials are often specified for kitchen and bath installations as well as for most office furnishings. Their durability, low maintenance, and, at least for the plastic laminates, their comparative inexpensiveness as a countertop material make them an excellent choice anywhere you don't want to worry about ruining wood. Moreover, they'll actually protect the custom cabinets you've built down below by keeping liquids away from the woodwork.

That's why every professional woodworker should have some familiarity with how to work plastic laminates and the newer solid surface materials. Even if you're a hobbyist, knowing how to work with these materials can save you money and open up your options. Working these materials isn't difficult, but because they're so different from wood, it helps to understand a little about them and the special tools and materials they require.

The Materials

The countertop material we see most commonly, like Wilsonart®, Formica®, and Micarta®, is made of kraft (grocery bag) paper saturated with melamine, the plastic that was used to make those unbreakable

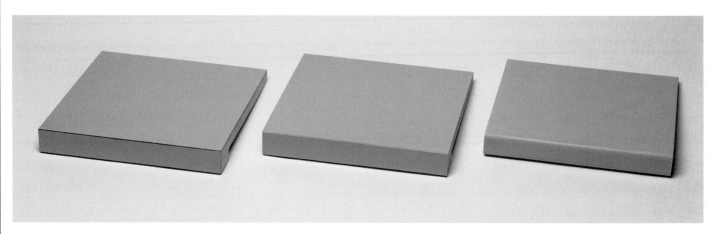

SYNTHETIC COUNTERTOP MATERIALS ARE DURABLE, VIRTUALLY MAINTENANCE-FREE, AND EASY TO WORK.
Plastic laminate with only its top layer colored is the least expensive (left), followed by laminate colored all the way through (center), which costs about three times as much. Solid surface materials (right) are more expensive yet, but look like natural stone and can be refurbished if scratched.

A CARBIDE-TIPPED SCORING TOOL MAKES CUTTING LAMINATE QUICK WORK. **When cutting a sheet of plastic laminate down to rough size, use a light touch for the first couple of passes. Increase pressure gradually until you're through the top layer.**

FOR A LESS-CONSPICUOUS SEAM **when using conventional plastic laminate, glue the edge on first, and then trim it flush with the top using a laminate trimmer or small router. That way, the top sheet of laminate will cover over the strip along the edge, making the seam less evident.**

plates from the '50s. Layers of this melamine-saturated kraft paper are then subjected to high temperatures and tremendous pressure, creating a dense, tough, brittle sheet. In most cases, the color and pattern of the sheet is only one layer thick and is determined by the color of the top sheet of paper. Laminate is most commonly sold in 4x8 sheets. This standard type of laminate (one layer of colored paper) generally retails for between $1 and $1.50 a sq. ft.

There are laminates available in which every layer of paper is colored. The advantage of this type of laminate is that seams at the edge of a countertop almost disappear because the color is consistent throughout the thickness of the laminate. The down side is that you'll pay up to three times as much for this aesthetic improvement—generally between $4 and $4.50 a sq. ft.

The solid surface materials (Gibraltar®, Corian®, Avonite®, Surell®, and Fountainhead®) consist of acrylic and/or polyester resins, depending on the brand, mixed with fillers and coloring agents. They usually come in ½-in. sheets, 31 in. by 145 in. (an inch over 12 ft.) but may also be cast into sinks or moldings at the factory. Solid surface material typically costs between $15 and $20 a sq. ft.

Working with Plastic Laminates

As when using wood veneers, you should cover both sides of the substrate to prevent warping due to uneven moisture transfer. An inexpensive noncolored laminate called backer board is sold exclusively for this purpose. If, however, the substrate is secured to a strong supporting framework, this step may be skipped.

The materials used most commonly as a substrate for plastic laminates are particleboard, medium-density fiberboard (MDF), and plywood. Laminates are usually bonded to the substrate with contact cement, although white glue also works well. In kitchen-cabinet factories and other large operations, the contact cement is usually sprayed, but for the hobbyist or small-shop professional, a knobby roller made especially for applying contact cement or a serrated squeegee will do just fine. I prefer the knobby rollers, which you can find in most places where laminate is sold.

When covering a countertop with laminate, you can either edge the countertop with wood or use the same material on the edge that you did on the top. If you're going to use wood, wait until after you have the laminate on the top trimmed flush with the edge before you glue and clamp the edge to the substrate. But if you're going to use laminate on the edge, you'll want to glue it on first, trim it flush, and then do the top (see the photo at right on p. 41). The idea is to make the seam as inconspicuous as possible.

Cut plastic laminate oversize: Trimming to exact size is done after the laminate is glued to the substrate, using a laminate trimmer or other small router with a bearing-guided, flush-trimming router bit.

You can cut plastic laminate to rough size on the table saw. Carbide-toothed, triple-chip blades work best, but as long as you're cutting oversize, any blade will do. Another consideration on the table saw is to make sure the laminate can't slip under the table saw fence and mess up your cut. Clamping a piece of wood to the fence so that the wood is flush with the table will do the job.

Another way of getting plastic laminate down to rough size is to use a straightedge and a carbide-tipped scoring tool made expressly for the purpose (see the photo at left on p. 41). These knives are generally available wherever you can buy the laminate itself. To use this tool, score the laminate

lightly on the first couple of passes, and then exert increasing pressure for another few passes. All you need to do is get through the first layer of the laminate; then you can fold the sheet up and down, and it will break cleanly along the scored line like drywall or tile, for example.

Before applying any adhesive, make sure that both the back of the laminate sheet and the face of the substrate are clean. Even small bits of debris will keep the two surfaces from mating nicely. Once the mating surfaces are clean, spread contact cement on both of them, and let them dry until just barely tacky to the touch.

When the two surfaces touch, they will bond immediately and permanently, so it's important that the laminate be positioned exactly where it belongs. The best way to do this is to lay a number of Venetian-blind slats (thin wood slats will work in a pinch) on the substrate at 10-in. to 12-in. intervals. Then set the laminate on top of these, positioning it precisely. After checking to see that the laminate is properly positioned, carefully remove the slats starting from the center and working outward.

Gently lower the laminate to the surface as each successive slat is removed (see the photo at left). Once the top is down, you can ensure a good bond across the entire sheet by applying pressure to the surface with a hard-rubber roller or by pounding on a wooden block with a hammer. Make sure there are no air pockets.

Because the contact cement bonds immediately, you can trim the overhanging edges flush right away. If you need to trim farther into a corner than the laminate trimmer's baseplate will allow, cut the laminate with a hacksaw blade, and then finish trimming it with a file.

If you are using laminate for the front edge, it's best to chamfer the edges with a 7°-trimmer bit, which will give you a crisp edge but one that won't cut you.

VENETIAN-BLIND SLATS PERMIT PRECISE PLACEMENT of the top sheet of laminate when using contact cement (right). Starting with strips every 10 in. or so over the length of this section of countertop, the author removed all the slats left of center. Next, he works from the center out to the right, putting pressure on each section as he removes a slat, being careful to avoid creating air bubbles.

Face-Joining

MIXING THE SEAM ADHESIVE IS EASY. Seam kits provided by the manufacturer of the solid surface material are used to edge-join sheets of the material or build up stacks of the strips to create a thicker edge. The kits consist of a bag with both resin and catalyst inside, separated by a plastic clip. You just remove the clip, knead till thoroughly mixed, move the seam material to one side by scraping the bag against a bench edge, and clip and squeeze.

SPRING CLAMPS PROVIDE ADEQUATE PRESSURE FOR FACE-JOINING and will not starve the joint. Because solid surface materials are nonporous and very dense, tightening down on pipe or bar clamps could easily squeeze out all the seam material. Also, the seam material shrinks as it dries, so the spring clamps compensate for this by maintaining consistent pressure.

A KNOBBY CONTACT-CEMENT ROLLER IS PERFECT FOR SPREADING SEAM MATERIAL (below), ensuring an even coat of the right thickness.

Solid Surface Materials

These high-dollar countertop materials are most often made to look like natural stone, but they're also available in a variety of solid and flecked colors. Solid surface materials don't require a substrate, though sheets of it are usually mounted to the framework of a counter using dabs of silicone sealer. The silicone allows for the slight expansion and contraction of the solid surface material.

Solid surface materials can be cut or shaped with most woodworking tools. Inside corners should have a radius of at least ¼ in. to avoid stress fractures. Seams should be at least 1 in. from inside corners and 3 in. from sink cutouts. There should always be some supporting structure below a seam.

Sheets are joined and edges are built up using manufacturer–supplied seam kits in colors that essentially disappear when a seam is done right. These seam kits consist of a sealed plastic bag containing a catalyst and colored resin, separated by a plastic clip on the outside of the bag. When the clip separating these components is removed, you can mix them by simply kneading the bag in your hands until the contents are thoroughly blended. Then you move all the

seam material to one side of the bag, snip an opposite corner, and squeeze out the seam material as needed. I use the same kind of knobby roller to spread the seam material as I do the contact cement because it leaves a consistently thick layer of adhesive.

As the seam material dries, it shrinks, so normal bar, pipe, or speed clamps could loosen. I use spring clamps, which maintain

Edge-Joining

PACKING TAPE AND DOWELS HOLD AN EDGE JOINT TOGETHER while the seam material sets up. The dowels keep the tape out of the joint, and the tape, stretched taut across the joint, provides enough pressure to get the joint to fuse. A strip of tape beneath the joint keeps it from bonding to the plywood work surface.

A FLAT-BOTTOMED ROUTER BIT ELIMINATES MOST OF THE EXCESS OF DRIED SEAM MATERIAL. Sanding in stages down to 600 grit will clean up the rest and polish the surface to a nice luster.

a steady pressure on the joint. Another advantage of using spring clamps is that you can't overtighten them. Because of the nonporous nature of these solid surface materials, it isn't difficult to squeeze all of the bonding resin out of the joint if you use regular clamps.

To join these solid surface materials edge to edge, I clean the edges with alcohol and position the pieces about ⅛ in. apart. I squeeze a bead of the seam material between the two pieces that I'm joining, working it into the joint if necessary. Then I pull the joint tight by hand, making sure there is squeeze-out over the full length of the joint. I hold the joint together while the seam material is drying by laying small dowels or pencils along both sides of the joint and then stretching lengths of packing (or similar) tape tightly across the joint and over the dowels. There's sufficient elasticity in the tape that I can stretch it so that it will maintain tension on the joint.

After the seam material has dried thoroughly (45 minutes to an hour), I trim the hardened squeeze-out flush using a router with a flat-bottomed bit and two clearance blocks mounted to its baseplate. The seam sands out easily to a glossy finish using regular 600-grit wet-or-dry sandpaper, but a matte finish is generally recommended by the manufacturers because it hides scratches better.

KEN PICOU is a designer and woodworker in Austin, Texas.

Sources

The following companies manufacture synthetic countertop materials (regular laminate = L; colored laminate = CL; solid surface material = SSM). Product literature is available from all of them. Some have instructional materials on use and installation.

Ralph Wilson Plastics Co. Inc.
PO Box 6110
Temple, TX 76503-6110
800-433-3222
Products: Wilsonart (L), Wilsonart Solid Core (CL), Gibraltar (SSM)

DuPont Co., Corian Products
PO Box 80702, Room 1218
Wilmington, DE 19880-0702
800-426-7426
Product: Corian (SSM)

Formica Corp., Samples Division
1504 Sadler Circle South
Indianapolis, IN 46239
800-367-6422
Products: Formica (L), Colorcore (CL), Surell (SSM)

Avonite Inc.
1945 South Highway 304
Belen, NM 87002
800-428-6648
Product: Avonite (SSM)

International Paper, Nevamar Division
8339 Telegraph Road
Odenton, MD 21113
410-551-5000
Products: Nevamar (L), Fountainhead (SSM)

No-Hassle Panel Handling

BY SKIP LAUDERBAUGH

When you need big, flat panels that are stable, smooth, and ready to be cut, you just can't beat sheet goods. But moving plywood, melamine, or medium-density fiberboard (MDF) is a backbreaker. A single 4x8 sheet of ¾-in. MDF weighs almost 90 lb., and it's terribly awkward to maneuver, especially by yourself.

I used to think that schlepping panels by hand was a necessary evil in my cabinet-making business. Like many small-shop owners, I didn't have the space or the budget for material-handling equipment like a forklift. I stored panels near my saw in a stack. But it seemed whichever panel I wanted was always buried at the bottom of the pile. The day I needed a panel that was

under 30 sheets of melamine, I just knew there had to be a better way.

It was time to stand back and analyze my entire panel-handling process—from unloading the truck to pushing panels through the saw. My goal was to devise a way for one person to unload, store, sort, and move panels to the saw, using the least possible effort. So I came up with a storage system built around a low platform.

Panel-Storage System Saves Labor, Space, and Time

When I began studying how I had been moving sheet goods, I realized how inefficient I'd been. So I designed a panel-storage system to achieve five basic objectives:
- provide easy access to panels
- minimize lifting of entire sheets
- work at safe, comfortable positions
- organize panel cutoffs
- make the most of my floor space

At the heart of the panel-handling system is a 4-ft. by 10-ft. platform. The top of the platform is 24 in. above the floor, which is easy on the back for those rare times that I have to lift an entire sheet. The top is also at the right height for sliding sheets directly off the tailgate of my truck. And by standing on the platform, I can leaf through panels or reach up to my overhead cutoff rack. Connected to the top are two panel supports (I call them bolsters) that slide in tracks. The bolsters can be removed for loading panels or adjusted to fit the stack of sheets as it grows or shrinks.

I store panels with the long edges on the platform and the faces leaning against the wall. To sort through the stack, I lean unwanted panels against the bolsters and leaf through the rest like pages in a book. The end of the platform is 6 ft. from the front of my saw, providing plenty of cutting room. But I can still rest an end of a sheet either on the saw table or on the platform. To maximize floor space, I built two low assembly tables that roll under the platform.

1. PLATFORM IS AT A COMFORTABLE HEIGHT FOR UNLOADING. The author slides plywood from his truck to the platform and tilts the panels up to the stack. He doesn't have to lift the full sheet.

2. BOLSTERS LET YOU LEAF THROUGH SHEET GOODS. When sorting through panels, two bolsters act like buttresses to support sheets at the front of the stack (left). The bolsters adjust by sliding and locking in tracks in the top of the platform (below). An overhead rack holds small cutoffs.

3. THE RIGHT SPACE BETWEEN SHEETS AND THE SAW. After the author selects a panel, he pulls it end first from the stack. The platform is 6 ft. from his saw so that both ends of the sheet can be supported.

4. PANEL SUPPORTED AT START OF CUT. The placement of the platform allows easy access to the saw and enables one person to move and cut panels. Leaving the front edge on the saw, the author feeds a panel into the blade by holding the unsupported back corner.

The No-Sweat Panel Shuffle

The beauty of the panel-handling system is that I almost never have to lift a full sheet. I either slide the panel or lift only one end. Photos 1 to 4 on p. 47 show my typical panel-moving sequence. If I do have to lift a sheet off the platform, a cutout makes it easy (see the photos below).

There are only four elements in my panel-storage system: the platform, the bolsters, the cutoff racks, and the assembly tables. I'll briefly explain how I built the platform, but I'll leave the specific measurements and details up to you. If you don't have headroom for overhead racks, for example, you can mount them somewhere else.

The platform The platform must be sturdy and big enough to hold 4x8 sheets. I designed the framework so I'd get the most storage area from the dead space underneath. I used 4x4s and 2x4s for the frame and secured it to a 10-ft.-long ledger I bolted to the wall. I anchored each leg of the platform to the floor.

The top of the platform has a pair of grooves running across the width, which serve as tracks for the adjustable bolsters. I bored ⅞-in.-dia. holes in the grooves every 6 in. to register the bolsters (the bolsters have alignment pins on the bottom) at various preset positions. And I sleeved the holes with short pieces of Schedule 40 PVC pipe to keep the holes from wearing and to keep the pins clean.

I let in and epoxied ⅛-in.-thick steel bars along both edges of the grooves to create lips to secure the bolsters. The bars protrude ⅜ in. into the groove, leaving a ⅝-in. gap between the bars. The top of the platform—¾-in. plywood covered by ¼-in. tempered hardboard—is screwed to the frame. On the wall behind the platform, I attached a ½-in. sheet of particleboard, so the panels have a flat surface to lean against.

The adjustable bolsters The bolsters measure 32 in. tall and are 9 in. wide at the bottom, tapering to 2 in. at the top. The cores are made of solid wood with ¾-in. plywood gussets glued and screwed to the sides. At the bottom of each bolster are two pins. One pin is a ½-in. carriage bolt that fits into the track holes to align the bolster; the other pin, also a ½-in. carriage bolt, is inverted and has a 1-in. flat washer under the head. This pin prevents uplift on the toe of the bolster as sheets are loaded against it. The pins are height adjustable, so they

STORED SHEETS ARE EASIER TO LIFT. When the author has to carry a full sheet, he lifts it upright to keep his back straight. A cutout gives his hand clearance to grab the sheet's lower edge.

engage both the holes and the lips of the track. Adjust the pins so they fit snugly in the tracks. Then carefully lean sheets against the bolsters to make sure they'll hold. You don't want a stack of sheets to crash against your legs later.

The cutoff racks Because I have a nice high ceiling, I made a rack above the platform for various-sized cutoffs. The overhead rack is divided into three sections. The left section holds 12-in.-wide pieces, the center 18-in.-wide pieces, and the right 24-in.-wide cutoffs. I located the bottom edge of the rack 62 in. above the platform to allow for 5-ft.-wide sheets and metric-sized plywood on the platform. The rack is attached to a ledger bolted to the wall. To the right of my platform is a storage rack that I use for wide cutoffs and long rippings. I can also use this area to store full panels vertically.

The roll-out assembly tables The space underneath the platform was the perfect place for storage-drawer units that also serve as cabinet-assembly tables. The two units are on wheels. They can be joined together to make one large surface, and when both tables are rolled under the platform, four drawers face out (see the photos at right). I keep fasteners and hardware in these. When I pull the tables out, there are plastic crates in the back where I store power tools. The crates slide out on pull-out shelves.

SKIP LAUDERBAUGH is a sales representative for Blum Hardware and a college woodworking instructor. His shop is in Costa Mesa, California.

DRAWERS MAKE USE OF FLOOR SPACE. A two-part assembly table rolls under the platform when not in use. Aligned by biscuits and clamped together, the table has slide-out bins in back.

Paint-Grade Cabinets

BY LARS MIKKELSEN

Most of us who work in wood love its color, grain, and texture, and we usually build to show off these characteristics. So when a client called and asked me to make a built-in stereo and display cabinet that had to be painted high-gloss white, I hesitated a little. But when I saw his house and the room the cabinet was to go in, it was obvious to me that paint was what this job called for. It is a modern house, sparsely furnished, with light-filled rooms defined by strong geometric forms. It was an excellent setting for a built-in cabinet that blends architectural and furniture detailing, and a good place for paint. Once I had accepted the logic of a paint finish, and also had accepted the job, every subsequent move I made was affected by the choice of finish—from decorative and structural decisions through selection of the materials to construction and sanding.

Planning for Paint

There are all grades of paint finishes, and it's important to have a clear idea of what you are aiming for before you begin. I talked with the client at length about the level to which the painting should be done. We wanted something well above the average wall-and-trim job, but taking it to the level of a grand piano would have made the cost

of the prep work and the painting prohibitive. So we agreed to try for something in between: A bit of grain texture might show under careful inspection, but the overall impression should be clean and unblemished. With an understanding of what we both expected, I was ready to begin.

When designing for a clear finish, the color and grain of the wood are often the central point. A big, flat panel can be spectacular if the grain is right, and curved grain along a focal axis can pull a piece together and make an otherwise very plain design a thing of beauty. All this is lost when you paint. What you gain in return is beautiful clean shadow lines, undisturbed by grain pattern and texture. Paint emphasizes the volume of intersecting planes, and I took advantage of this in the design of the cabinet. The piece was to be built into an alcove formed by a series of sharp-edged, squared-off arches that stepped out into the room. I adapted this step pattern for the cabinet's detailing, echoing and altering the step motif, playing off it without exactly reproducing it. I would have designed differently for a clear finish because the distinctive geometric patterns and proportions I settled on would have seemed cluttered and confused had they not been painted.

I try to design built-in furniture that looks truly built-in, like the beautiful buffets so often found in Victorian houses. Thinking of trim as an important design element contributes greatly to the integrated look that I always seek. It's easy, when designing built-in cabinets, especially painted ones, to fall into the trap of making misplaced kitchen cabinets. I try my best to avoid this by developing detailing that will give the piece a look of permanence, of belonging where it stands.

Because the piece was to be fairly big, I broke it down into four components that could be easily transported and assembled on site. I used a raised frame detail all around and between the major components. I applied these trim strips when the cabinets were set in place. This not only covered seams and edges but underscored the visual theme of the cabinet.

PICKING PAINT AS A FURNITURE FINISH IS NOT JUST A MATTER OF SHUFFLING COLOR SWATCHES. As Lars Mikkelsen discovered when he built these cabinets, painted work requires design decisions, materials, and preparation different from clear-finished work.

How to Pick Your Painter

To prequalify a painter for a difficult finishing job, I would recommend asking to see what he considers his finest work. I'd also ask him to explain in detail just how the finish will be achieved. I'd have him pre-finish one door panel using the materials and finish specified for the job. The client would approve that sample for color, gloss, smoothness of finish, and durability, and then it would be used as a job standard. I have often volunteered to do this when the situation warranted it, or when the client was unfamiliar with my work.

DAVE HUGHES is a professional finisher in Los Osos, California.

Drawer Detail

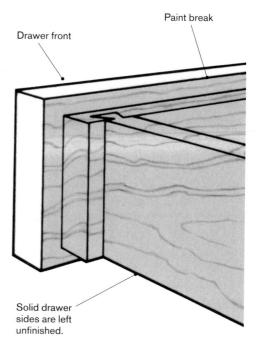

Drawer front

Paint break

Solid drawer sides are left unfinished.

Back of drawer fronts rabbeted to provide uninterrupted edge for transition from paint to raw wood.

To take advantage of the strong shadow lines, I made all the doors and drawers inset—flush with the surrounding surface—and free of exterior hardware. With inset doors and drawers, an even gap is always important, but when a black gap line is contrasted with white paint, small discrepancies become obvious to even the untrained eye. And I was making the tolerances small, so I needed hardware with fine adjustment. I wanted concealed European hinges for the doors and chose Grass® 1006 hinges on 20mm mounting plates. I picked the 1006 because it's relatively small; I was advised, though, that it won't work with inset doors that are any thicker than ¾ in. The doors are held closed and sprung open with Hafele™ touch-latches. For the drawers, I used Accuride full-extension slides and 1041 Flexa-Touch pushers. I purchased my hardware from Capitol Hardware® (see Sources on p. 57).

I wanted the doors painted on both sides, but for the drawers, I wanted only the fronts painted, leaving the solid-maple drawer boxes unfinished. This posed the problem of where to make the transition from painted surface to raw wood. I solved

it by running a rabbet around the inside edge of the drawer front, establishing a clean, uninterrupted line for the painter to tape off, as shown in the drawing above.

Materials to Fit the Finish

The materials I chose for this job were determined largely by their paintability. I needed something without open pores or great differences between hard and soft grain because such differences would telegraph through paint. I ended up choosing poplar for the solid wood and shop birch plywood. Both are relatively inexpensive, mill well and require minimal preparation for painting. Other choices for solid wood could be maple, birch, or alder. The main reason I chose poplar over the others was the ease with which it can be milled. For sheet goods, medium-density fiberboard is a possible choice; it paints nicely but is

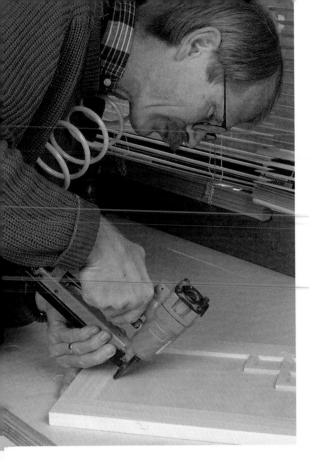

NAIL IN THE RAIL. The author shoots brads through the frame of the door to keep it from shrinking away from the panel, which could crack the paint and expose unfinished wood.

Speaker-Cabinet Door

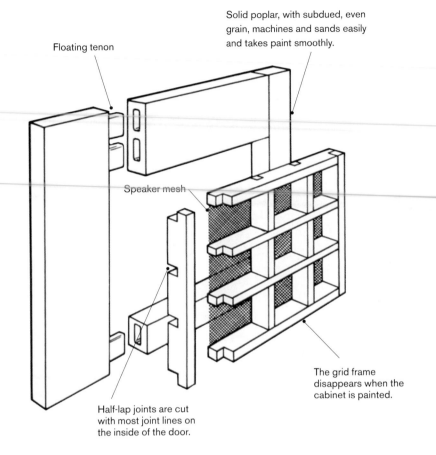

Floating tenon

Solid poplar, with subdued, even grain, machines and sands easily and takes paint smoothly.

Speaker mesh

The grid frame disappears when the cabinet is painted.

Half-lap joints are cut with most joint lines on the inside of the door.

extremely heavy to haul around and, there-fore, easy to damage.

Stereo speakers were to be housed behind the top doors on either side and the center door below. I made open-grid panels for those doors and covered them on the inside with sheets of metal speaker mesh (available from better stereo outlets). The mesh was painted to the same color as the cabinet and was easy to cut and install with small screws.

Joint Selection

Both the finish and the siting of the cabinet were factors in my selection of biscuits for its major joinery. Using biscuits alone on a freestanding piece that could take a lot of abuse over the years might not be a good idea; but once a built-in is in place and attached to the walls, there is not much stress on the joints. So I felt this technique would be amply strong. Because the sides of the cabinet would be hidden when it was

put in place, I used screws to draw the joints together while the glue set. I lipped all the plywood with ¾-in. by 1⅛-in. strips of solid poplar that I biscuited, glued, and nailed on. It saves a lot of time to nail the wood on rather than clamping it, and the spackled nail holes disappear under the paint. I also find that with nailing, I can locate the lipping exactly, but with clamps, the strips are a bit more difficult to control.

Though the carcase of a built-in does not take much abuse and you can use some shortcuts in its construction, this is not true for the doors and drawers. They need to be made with the same strength and care as for any freestanding piece. I made the drawer sides of solid wood, and then I joined them to the fronts with sliding dovetails.

I joined the stiles and rails of the doors with loose tenons. The mortises for these tenons I can cut with great precision on my

Spraying an Opaque Finish on Furniture

BY DAVE HUGHES

Ask any painter familiar with high-quality finishes and he or she will tell you that furniture-grade paint finishes are far more demanding than natural wood finishes. The simple reason is that the opaque surface of the paint highlights any defects or irregularities in grain and texture. Surfaces must be sanded, caulked, puttied, and re-sanded several times, and still some rubbing out and polishing may be required to achieve satisfactory results. The deeper the color and higher the gloss, the more demanding the process. With so many variables to be controlled, a patient, methodical approach is essential in applying opaque finishes.

Now, try to achieve that flawless finish inside a client's home, with kids, dogs, and neighbors dropping by for a look...to be candid, I didn't have too much enthusiasm for attempting the on-site finishing of Lars Mikkelsen's cabinets until I saw them for myself. They posed a real challenge, both technically and logistically, and that is what got me involved.

Prep the Work

On any on-site job, you have to take particular care to cover and to mask off all adjacent surfaces and any parts and hardware that won't be painted. The tape I use is Longmask by 3M®, a fine-creped blue tape with high tack that leaves no residue. I rub it down with a fingernail, and it provides an excellent edge seal, allowing no paint to creep underneath. With oil-based finishes, the tape can be pulled up when the paint is dry. With latex, which has greater bridging capacity, I score a line along a straight edge with a razor blade before removing the tape.

Good lighting is also critical for a top-quality paint job. Natural light is always best, but when I do use lamps, I place them far from the work to minimize glare.

The cabinets on Lars' job were already sanded quite smooth when I began work on them, but I always count on a certain added amount of time for re-sanding, puttying, and caulking because you can't really see the surface in detail until that first coat goes on. I have found it is best to fill all you can easily see; then apply a first coat of primer, and re-pair any small areas you have missed. The essential thing is to catch all of these before entering into the final-coats phase. This careful, methodical filling and sanding is where the patience factor really tells. For a fine finish, you must spend a certain amount of time just looking at every piece.

Lars had removed the doors, and I fitted each one with two small finish nails in the top and bottom edges (as shown in the drawing on the facing page) to act as stands for spraying, handling, and drying. Then I set up a makeshift booth in the garage to spray the doors and drawers.

Spray on Multiple Coats

The primer I sprayed was Sherwin-Williams® Hi-Build Lacquer Wood Surfacer reduced about 35% with medium- fast lacquer thinner. I used a high-volume, low-pressure (HVLP) spray unit, which, with its portability and reduced overspray, is particularly well-suited to on-site work. I used the HVLP unit with a Capspray® fine-finishing gun.

After spraying two coats of lacquer wood surfacer, I lightly sanded all surfaces with 400-grit wet-or-dry sandpaper that I first broke in on the backs of doors or bottoms of cabinets where dry-fall overspray accumulates. I turn the paper over and use the paper backing to abrade the knife-edges of doors, drawers, and trim to avoid burning through the finish.

The third coat of primer was a final fill-coat, not really sanded, but rubbed with the back of sandpaper for smoothness. Before every operation, I used a static-free tack-rag and blew the surfaces off with the air line on the spray gun. I allowed four hours between coats of primer because that's how long it took to spray a coat on the case and all the parts. But a lacquer undercoat is generally dry and ready to sand in 45 minutes to an hour, depending on the weather.

I applied two finish coats of Benjamin Moore IronClad® fast-dry industrial enamel, which has superior leveling-out characteristics and fast set-up time. The short tack time is critical when finishing on-site to minimize dust settling onto the finish. I thinned the enamel with about 30% xylol solvent and sprayed it at orifice settings between 0.006 and 0.009, something less than half the opening you would use to paint an ordinary wall.

Ready for Paint

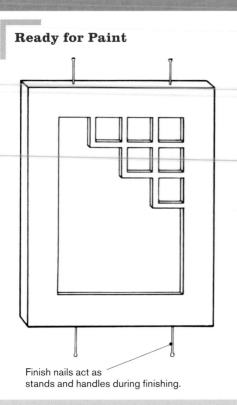

Finish nails act as
stands and handles during finishing.

I alternated between vertical, horizontal, and conical spray patterns as I worked to suit the intricate detailing on the cabinet doors, with the spray pressure just high enough to atomize the enamel. The Capspray gun enables me to spray in a cone pattern about the diameter of a pencil—it's practically an airbrush at that setting—which worked beautifully in the square decorative recesses of this cabinet. For the doors and frames, I switched to a 6-in. to 8-in. horizontal fan pattern.

A single coat was actually a two-step process. On the doors, for instance, I laid down a light tack-coat initially to cover the surface, rotated and tack-coated the back, and then flipped and rotated back for a full flowing coat. This method allows me to see how the material is performing and adjust viscosity, spray pattern, pres-

sure, and fluid levels before committing to a full coat. It also lets me lay down more material in one coat. I sanded lightly between coats of enamel with broken-in 600-grit paper, wiped down with a tack rag, and allowed 24 hours between coats. I applied a third coat to all the doors and countertops.

When the final coat on the doors had dried hard, I removed the nail stands, puttied the holes, and touched them up with two coats applied with an artist's brush. This was the only brushwork on the job.

Final Repairs and Sanding

After spraying the final coat, I took a few days away from the job before returning to do a final inspection and any necessary buffing out or touching up. The hiatus gave me some perspective and also let the finish cure hard and reach its final sheen. If you do any small repairs before the final sheen is reached, you may find they stand out later, looking either too glossy or too dull. I repair tiny blemishes by rubbing out with rottenstone or #00000 steel wool or buffing with alcohol and a tightly woven cotton cloth. A slow, hard rub with a coarser abrasive will give a matte finish while a fast, light stroke with a finer grit will yield a glossy one. By carefully adjusting the amount of pressure and the type of polishing compound, feathering out any touch-up areas and matching the sheen to the surrounding surface, you can approach a showroom finish with an on-site application.

mortise fixture. The solid doors have a ¼-in. birch-plywood panel sitting in a groove. It is important that this panel never move in the groove, and thus expose unpainted wood, so I nailed it in with a few brads, as shown in the photo on p. 53. The steps in these doors are strips of solid poplar ½ in. wide by ¼ in. thick, half-lapped and glued in place. The open grids for the speaker cabinets are made with ½-in.-wide by ¾-in.-thick pieces of solid poplar, half-lapped at every joint, as shown in the drawing on p. 53. Had these doors been left clear, I probably would have mortised the end of each crosspiece of the grid into the stiles and rails. But because no grain would show, I made the grid as an independent unit with a frame of its own, with all half laps, and then glued up the stiles and rails around it.

Paint Prep

It would be hard to find someone who really loves filling and sanding, but the job can be made easier and less tedious by doing as much as possible as you build. For many parts, it's much simpler and quicker to do the prep work before assembly. I carefully filled and sanded the plywood panels in the solid doors before glue-up. On all the pieces of lipped plywood for the carcase, I sanded the wood flush to the plywood with a belt sander that I slowed down with an electronic speed control. The slow speed makes this operation much easier and safer. Next, I inspected all the pieces carefully and then filled and sanded any little cracks or dings that might show up later. Remember that paint really magnifies these blemishes.

When the carcases were assembled, I applied white latex caulk to all the many corners whether I could see a seam or not. I used spackle for any joint or surface that would be sanded. All this filling must be done carefully because even a hairline crack will show horribly once the paint is on. To

EVEN WITH END GRAIN, IT'S BEST TO SCRAPE OFF MOST OF THE SPACKLE. **If necessary, apply a second time rather than build up a thick layer. Do a last round of filling when the piece has been primed. The layer of finish will highlight any imperfections.**

achieve clear, crisp lines and joints, it is important to press caulk into the cracks but immediately remove all excess, leaving interior corners square rather than forming a little cove of caulk. To do this, I laid down as small a bead of caulk as possible. Then I used a putty knife that I had filed down so that it came to a knife edge and its corners were sharp and square. I probably removed 95% or more of the caulk that I applied. I don't worry about small smears of caulk or glue, but all protrusions should be removed.

After gluing up the doors, I caulked all around the groove and panel joint, cleaning it up with my putty knife. I filled the seams between the grid pieces with spackle, as shown in the photo on the facing page. When there's a long run to fill, it's easier to lay down a bead of caulk, but in tight spaces like the grids, caulk will make a mess. It is important to work methodically at this, so as not to miss any of the little seams. Then I took all the doors to be thickness-sanded. Some cabinet shops offer this service, and it is very worthwhile. It saves time while doing a superior job, keeping everything wonderfully flat, resulting in a beautiful, clean reflection of light when painted.

At this point, all parts had been made, filled, and sanded, and all I needed to do in the shop was to fit the doors and drawers in their openings. Before fitting anything, I assembled the four individual carcases, screwing them together and shimming them as needed to get everything straight, flat, and square. I glued my shims in place so that they would stay on one of the carcases. That way, when I later assembled the carcases on site, I was sure to get them exactly the way they were when I fitted the doors and drawers, saving a lot of frustration and awkward planing. I then sanded everything down to 180 grit with my random-orbit sander and broke all sharp edges by hand-sanding, creating a small roundover. A roundover always looks nice, but when painting, it is absolutely essential because paint will not adhere to sharp edges and a dark line will appear.

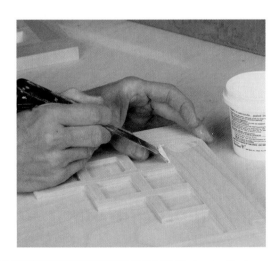

FILL EVERY CORNER, WHETHER YOU CAN SEE A SEAM OR NOT. **For long runs, caulk is best, but in tight quarters, like the door panel grids, the author uses spackle because it's less messy. With a freshly filed putty knife, he removes 95% of the filler he lays down.**

Installation

Now the moment of truth. No matter how many times I have done installation, it is still stressful until everything is in place. This time everything went smoothly, and the major components were quickly set and screwed together. I then shifted the unit around a bit in the wall opening to get all side margins as even as possible. I removed all doors, drawers, and hardware, numbering all the hinges so that I could put them back where they came from. This makes re-installation much faster because almost no fine-tuning is needed. I left the drawer guides in place and then covered them with tape.

Though this is the point when I hand a job off to the painter, I always make certain to return when the piece has been primed. With the first coat on, previously unnoticed flaws can readily be seen, and it is the last chance to repair them without having to repaint everything. In this case, there was nothing for me to do at the priming stage because the painter had already done any filling that was needed. I always insist on re-hanging the doors and hardware myself: This is not a painter's job, and he or she cannot be expected to do it so that the doors fit properly.

The Payoff

Finally, everything was done, and I could see the piece the way I had imagined it while doing the design. I was hoping my client would be as happy as I was. I got a clue when I returned for my check and found the furniture rearranged. Before, it had been facing the fireplace, and now it all faced the cabinet.

LARS MIKKELSEN is a professional cabinetmaker living in Santa Margarita, California.

Sources

Capitol Hardware
1519 Riverside Ave.
Paso Robles, Calif.
93446
805-238-7669

Solid-Wood Edging for Plywood

BY STEVEN COOK

A LIGHTLY BOWED CAUL, faced with felt, needs only a few clamps to apply even pressure on plywood edging.

Plywood cabinets are great: strong, quickly assembled, and relatively light. But what do you do with all those raw edges? Veneer tape is certainly the easiest way to cover an edge, but I've found that sooner or later the tape chips and frays. An edge made of ¾-in.-sq. stock stays put, but it looks clunky, especially around a cabinet door. I experimented with a number of ways of concealing plywood edges before finding one I liked.

I now use 3/16-in.-thick edging and glue it to the plywood before the cabinets are assembled. The look is clean and sophisticated, and the quality of the finished product is obvious. It's sold many jobs for me.

The secret to using such thin edging successfully is in the clamping. The glueline must be even and free of gaps. Rather than using heavy cauls held flat with many clamps, I use light bowed cauls faced with dense felt. A clamp on each end of the panel is all I need because flattening the bow presses the felt face against the edging from end to end of the panel. I get a clean, even

FINISH THE EDGES OF A DOOR WITH A 3/16-IN. ROUNDOVER BIT. Run the sides by the top and bottom to cover the end grain.

glueline with a minimum of trouble (see the photo at left on the facing page).

In my shop, I have four cauls 3 ft. long, four 1½ ft. long, and two 8 ft. long. This is ample for gluing up the edging on an average kitchen-cabinet job. The cauls are handy for all kinds of clamping operations; I find myself reaching for them often.

Make Cauls from Bowed Stock or Laminations

All I need to make a bowed caul is stock that's about 1 in. sq. and lightly bowed. A curve of about ½ in. over 3 ft. works fine. A little more than that is fine, but if the curve is much less, the caul will not exert enough pressure for an even glueline.

I use stock that's too warped for anything else—like offcuts I get from straightening bowed edges or pieces that take up a curve after being sawn. If I have no warped lumber, then I laminate four ¼-in. layers of scrap to make cauls. I glue up the strips over a form with yellow glue to create a curve.

I can't find any functional difference between these two kinds of cauls, but trying to cut the cauls out of straight stock on a bandsaw isn't a good idea. It's difficult to saw a curve without creating bumps and hollows. Uneven spots in the face of the caul will prevent it from being held tightly against the edging all along its length. So a sawn caul requires a lot of extra planing and sanding. By using planed laminates bent around a simple form, I can get a perfectly fair curve that requires no additional smoothing.

The dense felt I glue to the cauls is something I use in piano repair. It's called back-rail cloth, and it pads the rails that piano keys sit on while at rest. The felt is about ¼ in. thick and is sold in rolls 1½ in. wide by 52 in. long. I buy it from Pacific Piano Supply. A roll costs $7, and Pacific Piano has a $25 minimum. (Also, a piano tuner probably has some felt and may be willing to sell a few feet.) I glue the felt to

the convex side of the caul with yellow glue. When the caul is dry, I clamp it, felt side down, on a scrap of plywood and trim the excess felt with a razor blade or X-Acto® knife.

Apply and Trim the Edging

I apply edging to plywood before the cabinet boxes are assembled. For an average-sized kitchen, I figure on 20 bd. ft. of wood for ³⁄₁₆-in.-thick strips. I usually make the edging from the same species of wood as the cabinets, but I have used contrasting

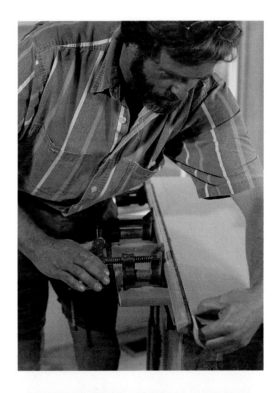

IF THE EDGING IS ⅛ IN. WIDER THAN THE PLYWOOD, then the alignment is not crucial. You can trim the overhang later.

FINGER PULLS ARE DEEPER THAN STANDARD EDGING, so make the bottom edging thick enough to accommodate them.

Sources

Pacific Piano Supply
16153 Leadwell
Van Nuys, CA 91406
818-779-1586

RUN THE ROUTER IN A CLIMB CUT **(from right to left) to prevent tearout. It leaves a rough edge, so follow with a block plane.**

colors on occasion. Maple and walnut, for instance, look great together.

I dimension my edging stock so that it overhangs the plywood by ¹⁄₁₆ in. on each edge. Having the edging wider makes it easy to cover the plywood edge without having to worry about careful alignment during clamping (see the top photo on p. 59).

I run the stock through the tablesaw, cutting the strips thicker than I need. Then I take them down to ³⁄₁₆ in. with a planer, cutting both sides to get clean, parallel-sided strips. I always use yellow glue for edging simply because it's easy to use and holds up well. If the caul is long, I put a clamp in the middle to hold it and then one on each end. Twenty minutes is all the job needs—just long enough for the glue to tack. I get into a nice rhythm—gluing, clamping, unclamping, and on to the next. It's a good time to listen to music.

The glue can continue to cure un-clamped; just be sure to wait several hours before trimming the edges flush. For that, I use a router with a flush-trimming bit (see the photo at left). If you run the router in the usual way—from left to right as you face the panel—the edge might tear out, possibly to a point below the edge of the plywood. To prevent this, I run the router the "wrong way" in what's known as a climb cut.

Climb cutting can be risky, but by using a bit with a bearing and by keeping the overhang to less than ⅛ in., it's easy to keep the router under control. A climb cut tends to be a little rougher than a push cut, but a light pass with a handplane will leave the joint absolutely flush (you can do all the trimming with a plane, if you like). Then I trim the ends to length with a fine-toothed Japanese saw and a file.

Try a Roundover Bit for Doors

I like the look of thin edging on a door when it has been finished with a ³⁄₁₆-in.-radius roundover bit (see the photo at right on p. 58). Doing this hides the glueline and makes it easier to hang the door because the rounded line is visually more forgiving. If a hinge has to be pulled out to true up a warped door, your eye isn't drawn to the slight unevenness. You can chamfer the edge right up to the glueline, but that creates a hard shadow that tends to draw the eye to any place slightly out of parallel.

Finger pulls can be routed into the door edge very easily. Simply plan ahead by making the edging deep enough to accommodate the cove bit you'll use for the detail (see the bottom photo on p. 59).

STEVEN COOK is an instrument- and cabinetmaker who has been making his living at woodworking for more than 25 years.

Dressing Up Plywood Cabinets with Face Frames

BY JOSEPH BEALS

One of the first face frames I built was a nightmare at every step. It was a maple behemoth, more than 11 ft. long, for a row of cabinets I had built at the job site. When I glued up the frame in my shop, the dowel joints would not line up until I fairly beat them together. I applied the finished frame on site just as a thunderstorm blew in. I spread white glue on the back of the frame and used two hands, two knees, and my forehead to hold it in place. A lightning bolt took out the power at about the third nail. As I set the frame by kerosene lamp, I decided face frames must be the nastiest job invented.

I have made plenty of face frames since then, and they don't seem nearly as difficult anymore. I now make them with mortise-and-tenon joints and attach them to carcases with biscuits or with counterbored and plugged screws.

FACE FRAMES COMPLETE A CABINET. The author fits a face frame to a plywood carcase, giving the cabinet the appearance of solid-wood furniture.

How a face frame is made is no more important than how it's designed. Face frames should be a subtle element in the composition of a cabinet. A face frame that draws attention to itself through awkward proportions or wild grain isn't doing its job.

And no matter how face frames are made, they all do the same thing. A solid-wood face frame provides a finished front on case work that's usually made of some manufactured material such as plywood or fiberboard. The frame covers the raw edges and provides a place to hang doors, fit drawers, and attach trim. Face frames are appropriate for a variety of practical, built-in, and free-standing furniture.

Design Face Frames Like Doors

Parts of a face frame are best put together as if they were a conventional door frame: Outer stiles should run full height, with top and bottom rails let in between. Internal partitions should follow the same pattern (see the drawing below).

These rules serve well in most instances, but they should be modified when a pair of face frames are joined end to end. The joint between them will look best if the top and bottom rails butt into each other, rather than into side-by-side stiles. This will give the illusion of a continuous frame, which looks better.

Guidelines for Designing Face Frames

Start with a basic width of 1¾ in. for rails, stiles, and partitions, and vary it according to the rules below.

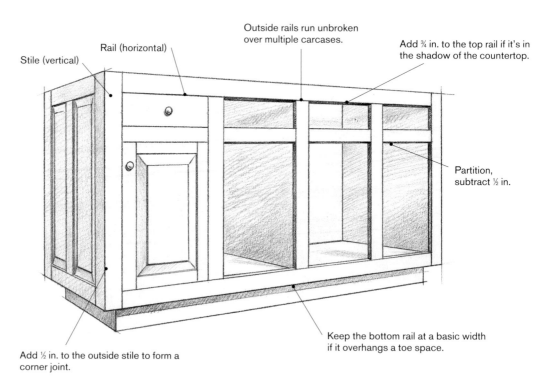

Stile (vertical)

Rail (horizontal)

Outside rails run unbroken over multiple carcases.

Add ¾ in. to the top rail if it's in the shadow of the countertop.

Partition, subtract ½ in.

Add ½ in. to the outside stile to form a corner joint.

Keep the bottom rail at a basic width if it overhangs a toe space.

Memory tip: Cabinet stiles go up and down, like the hem styles of women's dresses.

It's important to use straight-grained, stable stock for face frames. Wild grain should be avoided, even when the rail or stile is fastened along its length, such as along a cabinet bottom. It will draw the eye to a pattern that probably has no symmetry or other resolution. The frame should not compete visually with the doors and drawers it surrounds.

There are no best dimensions for the various rails, stiles, and partitions, just some guidelines to keep them visually balanced. I mill rough 4/4 stock to $^{13}/_{16}$ in., but standard ¾-in. stock is fine. The parts should be neither so wide as to appear clumsy nor so narrow as to seem fragile. The proportions of smaller parts such as drawer partitions should be reduced to keep them from looking oversized. For a face frame that will house flush-mounted doors and drawers, I find 1¾ in. to be the most satisfying width for ordinary stiles, and I derive other component dimensions from it.

Outside stiles need to be wider at corners because they form a joint. To make both appear 1¾ in. wide and maintain symmetry around the corner, one must be cut down to 1 in. wide or less. Working with such a narrow piece is not worth the effort, especially if grooved for a panel. I widen the front stile to 2¼ in. and make the side stile 1½ in. wide. (For more on how to get around a corner, see the drawing at right.)

You Have Several Assembly Choices

There are at least four ways to make a face frame: with dowels, biscuits, pocket screws, or more traditional mortise-and-tenon joinery. Your choice will probably depend on what tools you have on hand and which method you have experience with. For me, the best approach is the old-fashioned way—the mortise and tenon—even if it takes a little longer and is a little more complicated (see the sidebar on pp. 64-65).

Mortise-and-tenon joints are strong, very reliable, and easily made. They give positive, foolproof alignment of parts. To cut mortises, I use a small slot mortising machine. You could use a router, which is also very fast and accurate.

I make the mortises about ⅜ in. deep and about ⁵⁄₁₆ in. wide. It's not necessary to make them deeper because a face frame is not subject to particularly severe loading. They should be easy to put together but without too much play (see the sidebar on pp. 66-67).

When all the joints have been cut, I dry-fit the face frame and compare it to measurements on my drawings and the carcase. It helps to imagine the finished cabinet and overlay that mental picture on the face frame, in case something brutally obvious has slipped through the design process. If all is well, I glue it together.

I brush yellow glue in the mortises and on the tenons and fit the frame together across sawhorses. I clamp across all joints with just enough pressure to bring the tenon shoulders home tight, checking once again to make sure the joints are flat. Adjustments can be made by shifting a clamp or moving it to the opposite side. However, unlike a door, a face frame does not need to be perfectly flat. Because it's relatively thin, the frame will be fairly limber and will be drawn flat when fitted to the carcase. I also check each joint for square and lateral alignment, adjusting them with a hammer and block if necessary.

I measure diagonals to check the face frame for square. This is crucial but easy to forget. To square a slightly racked face frame, I skew each clamp slightly. If that doesn't work, I add a clamp across the long diagonal to pull it into place. Despite every care, the square of the door and drawer openings on a complex face frame may not agree with the overall squareness of the frame. When this happens, I split the difference.

Turning a Corner

As seen from the top, face frames can be joined at a cabinet corner in several ways.

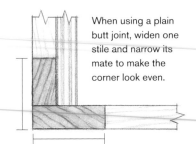

When using a plain butt joint, widen one stile and narrow its mate to make the corner look even.

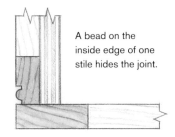

A bead on the inside edge of one stile hides the joint.

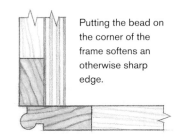

Putting the bead on the corner of the frame softens an otherwise sharp edge.

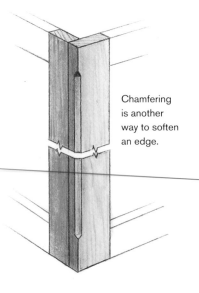

Chamfering is another way to soften an edge.

Attach Face Frame to Carcases

Whenever possible, I attach the face frame in my shop because all my tools are nearby, and clamping a frame to a cabinet is much easier when the cabinet can be parked on a couple of sawhorses. Attaching them on site is an option if the carcases and frames are too big to carry as a single unit. Attaching a face frame to carcases after they've been set in place is my last option, though there are circumstances when it's the best method.

No matter where you end up attaching face frames, the single most demanding detail is keeping the top edge of the bottom rail flush with the inside of the cabinet bottom. (One exception is when the cabi-

Three Common Ways to Build a Frame

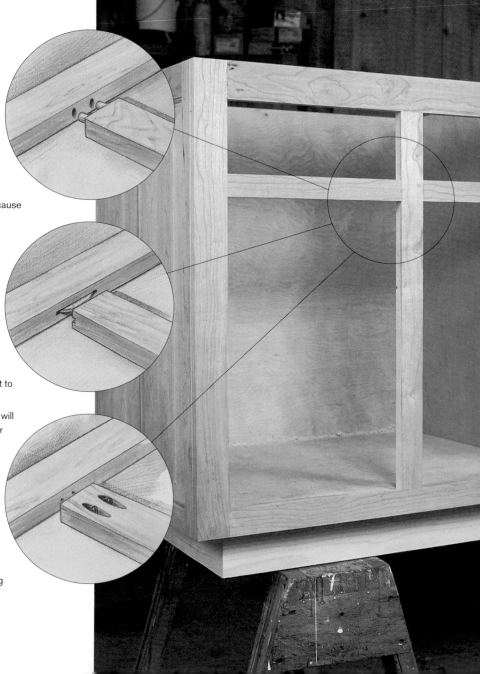

Face-frame joints don't need to be particularly strong, but they should go together easily and be simple to align. Mortise-and-tenon joinery is traditional, but face frames can also be assembled with dowels, biscuits, or pocket screws.

Dowels

PROS: Doweled face frames are easy to lay out because you don't need to figure in tenon lengths.

CONS: To prevent frame pieces from rotating, each joint requires two dowels, which can be difficult to align accurately. Once drilled, dowel holes can't be adjusted to compensate for even the smallest alignment mistakes during assembly. If used with yellow glue, doweled joints must be pressed tight at one go: a lapse of a minute or less will let a dowel seize with the joint open.

Biscuits

PROS: Biscuit joints are the fastest and easiest joint to make. They align quickly and positively.

CONS: Kerfs for the smallest standard-sized biscuit will break through and show on edges of stock narrower than 2⅜ in. If a molding detail will be added to the inside of the face frame, biscuits may be the most convenient joinery choice.

Pocket screws

PROS: Pocket screws on the back of the frame make a fast and simple joint.

CONS: Joints are difficult to align perfectly flat and can't be adjusted in any practical manner during assembly without pulling out screws. A dedicated jig is needed to drill screw holes.

net bottom becomes a door stop.) The veneers on most cabinet-grade plywoods are very thin and will not withstand much planing or sanding. The top edge of the bottom rail must, therefore, be fastened dead flush or a fraction proud to permit finishing to a smooth joint. This joint has always been particularly important to me. I think it's a sign of sloppy work when it's not flush, but others may not be so obsessed.

Shop installation with biscuits and clamps When I attach face frames in the shop, I use biscuits almost exclusively. The biscuit joint is strong, accurate, and doesn't show. Also, biscuits are invaluable along the bottom rail, which demands accurate

Attaching Frames on the Job Site

It's often easier to apply face frames while cabinets are still in the shop, but very large or long cabinets are a different story. When a number of smaller cabinet components are put together on a job site, they can be joined with a common face frame. In that situation, frames can be attached to the cabinets with screws or nails.

Plugged screws

PROS: Plugged screws are useful when clamping a biscuit joint is not an option. They are the equal of biscuits for strength and overall convenience and can be used with biscuits for better alignment. Use 1⅝-in. black drywall screws through a 1³⁄₁₆-in.-thick face frame. They grip well in plywood and do not require a pilot hole.

CONS: The plugs show if the cabinet is finished bright.

Nails

PROS: The oldest and simplest method is glue and nails, especially for painted work. Nail holes are small and can be filled easily.

CONS: Nails will sometimes wander sideways in a plywood edge, shifting the face frame. Occasionally, a nail will split the plywood or pop out of a cabinet side. Nailed frames are difficult to align exactly without biscuits.

65

positioning. However, it's foolish to trust the biscuit to align everything perfectly because there can be some occasional play in the slots. Even with biscuits, you should expect to make adjustments.

In some materials, such as medium-density fiberboard, biscuits may be the only practical attachment because screws hold poorly in the edge and tend to split the material. Although biscuits allow me to eliminate screws entirely, the disadvantage is that I need to use clamps. Clamps tie up the carcase for at least an hour, and they always get in the way of cleaning off glue that squeezes out of the joints.

On-site installation with plugged screws For a very long run of cabinets, on-site installation of face frames has some benefits. Long runs of cabinets look better when united with a single face frame, but attaching them all in the shop and moving them to the site later is impractical. Multiple cabinets should be set in place individually, then fastened together to ensure they're square, plumb, and aligned.

Shop installation of face frames is convenient because the cabinets can lie on their backs, which gives full access for clamping. On site, after the cabinets are set against the walls, clamping access disappears.

My Way of Making Face Frames

USE MORTISE-AND-TENON JOINERY for a strong, easily aligned joint. To save time, cut the tenon shoulders on the table saw without changing the blade height.

BEFORE GLUE-UP, dry-fit the whole frame. This ensures all pieces will go together smoothly when coping with glue that sets quickly and an armload of clamps.

SAWHORSES MAKE CLAMPING UP EASY. They'll let you fit clamps on both sides of the frame for even clamping pressure.

In this application, counterbored, plugged screws are hard to match for strength and overall convenience. Once they're in, the attachment is done. Screws grip well in plywood and do not require a pilot hole in the plywood edge.

To hide the screws, I use plugs cut from the same stock as the face frame. For bright finished work, I try to match grain pattern and color as well. After the glue dries, I strike off most of the excess plug with a chisel and watch how the grain runs. If the grain runs down into the plug, some of the plug can pop off below the surface, leaving a tedious repair job. To avoid it, I finish paring off the plug from the other direction.

Plugged holes vanish under paint, but even with careful grain and color matching, that little circle is always visible under a bright finish. This isn't necessarily offensive, but it requires that screw holes be carefully and symmetrically aligned. I find that there is something pleasing about a thoughtful, geometric pattern of plugs along the edges of a face frame.

JOSEPH BEALS is a custom woodworker in Marshfield, Massachusetts.

BISCUITS ARE BEST. Although strong, biscuits can be difficult to align when the face frame hangs over the edge of the cabinet. Instead of resetting the fence on his biscuit joiner, the author uses a spacer block the thickness of the overhang to align the tool.

CLAMP-UP IS A CINCH with the carcase on its back. Face frames attached with biscuits need to be clamped. Sawhorses make it easy to reach all the edges of the carcase and face frame.

ONLY PERFECT RECTANGLES HAVE EQUAL DIAGONALS. The author compares diagonals to make sure the face frame is square. Angling the clamps corrects minor problems.

Fine Furniture from Plywood

BY
MARK EDMUNDSON

INCORPORATING CUSTOM THICKNESSES, matched grain and seams, and solid-wood details will help shopmade furniture beat the plywood box look.

Selecting Sheet Goods

SOME OF THE FINEST LOGS end up as plywood veneers. Most hardware plywood dealers sell attractive sheet goods in a variety of common species, featuring rotary-sliced, book-matched, and quarter-sawn veneers.

Woodworkers can choose from a wide selection of hardwood plywood. Whatever you want is likely to be available somewhere, especially if you live in a city. And if your dealer doesn't have it in stock, the dealer can order it from a supplier. Most places carry a pretty good selection of ¼-in.-thick hardwood plywood (another reason to use my sandwich system rather than ¾-in.-thick plywood). If you're forced to order something sight unseen, try to be as specific as you can about your needs. Most places will let you decline something if it's not up to your expectations.

You'll most likely have to make decisions about veneer slice, core type, face grade, and back grade. I put the highest value on the veneer slice, which is the manner in which the veneer has been cut. The best choices for the exterior are either a plain-sliced or quarter-sliced veneer. Both of these are cut in a straight line, duplicating the figure of sawn lumber. Rotary slicing involves centering the log in a lathe and turning it against a broad cutting knife. The grain pattern does not match that typically found in solid wood.

For a hardwood plywood core, I prefer MDF because there's no chance of a void being telegraphed onto the surface veneers. The face grade will most likely be A if you've chosen plain- or quarter-sliced veneer. It's also helpful to know that veneer-core plywood tends to run a little under its stated size, usually by a

One look at a stack of hardwood plywood and you know why there are fewer and fewer nice planks in a unit of lumber. The best logs are scooped up by veneer mills, ending up in kitchen cabinets and mass-produced entertainment centers. Wanting to rescue these attractive panels, I had to find a way to turn them into pieces my clients would accept as custom furniture. The freestanding cabinet featured here incorporates many of the techniques I've developed for overcoming the inherent drawbacks of using plywood.

By laminating ¼-in.-thick panels around a core of medium-density fiberboard (MDF), I create custom panels that are thicker than the standard ¾ in. This technique also allows me to contrast the exterior wood with a different interior species—in the cabinet

shown here I used cherry and maple. I also locate the veneer seams carefully to create a solid-wood effect. The solid legs, corner posts, and door frames add to the furniture feel. Other custom touches include the raised-panel treatment on the plywood door panels and the mitered edge-banding on the top and bottom. The top also has a raised lip, or "pencil roll," applied at the back edge. An attractive drawer box, custom door pulls, and nice hinges complete the piece.

Plywood Can Overcome Its Deficiencies

While plywood presents a number of problems to the custom furniture maker, it also offers the solutions. The hardwood plywood at a lumber dealer is probably "A-1," which refers to a grading system. On the A side, you'll find very impressive veneers, all

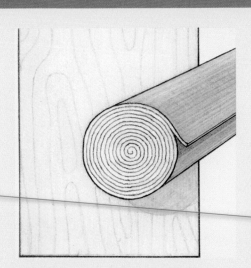

Rotary-sliced veneer plywood looks the least like solid lumber. The veneer is peeled off the perimeter of the log, producing a wavy pattern that doesn't exist in solid wood.

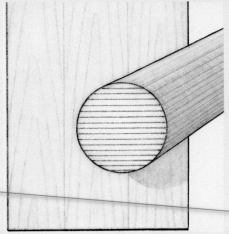

Plain-sliced veneer plywood is a better choice. The veneer is sliced as plainsawn lumber would be, giving the appearance of solid wood. It is often book-matched at its seams.

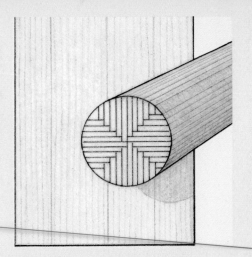

Quarter-sliced veneer looks like quarter-sawn lumber. Both are sliced parallel to the growth rings. Quartersawn oak plywood with book-matched ray flecks has added appeal.

continued on pp. 70–71

It's a shame not to utilize the wonderful veneers that end up on sheet goods.

book-matched and ready for sanding. But the other side (the "1" side) is usually uninspiring, consisting of veneers with sap and from different logs or flitches. Even if you put this side on the inside of a cabinet, it still detracts from the overall quality and appeal.

At some point I came up with the idea of sandwiching ¼-in.-thick A-1 on both sides of an MDF core. The idea allows me to get rid of the inconsistent side and gives me the freedom to choose an alternative wood for the interior of a cabinet, something I usually do when I cut my own veneers. Also, the center core can be whatever thickness I want, further distancing a piece from the plywood-box look. Last, plywood is much easier to laminate onto a substrate than thin veneer is.

Avoiding the ¾-in. edge thickness is important on the top and bottom as well as on the sides of a cabinet like this. I like the top to be at least 1 in. thick. An even thicker bottom gives a piece a sturdy and substantial feel. In this case I wanted to use applied feet, so the thicker bottom allowed more purchase for the joinery. The core MDF is ½ in. or thicker, and I often glue up the core from thinner MDF plies. For the bottom of this cabinet, I used one ⅜-in.-thick ply and one ¼-in.-thick ply to achieve a ⅝-in.-thick core, an overall thickness of 1⅛ in.

Treat the plywood veneers as you would solid wood. Use to your advantage the grain orientation, the position of veneer seams, the book-matches and the runs of veneers from the same flitch. For this cabinet I was able to line up the veneer seams on the sides and top so that the grain appears

Selecting Sheet Goods

MDF- VS. VENEER-CORE PLYWOOD. Veneer core tends to run a little undersized, while MDF core is usually right on.

light ¹⁄₃₂ in., while MDF core is usually dead on.

I make it a point to talk with a knowledgeable sales clerk and view everything the yard has to offer. You may find a few nice alternatives or surprises.

As you leaf through a stack of plywood, you'll notice that the sheets come in runs, that is, there will be several sheets with veneers from the same log, or flitch. This run might be two or five sheets long. If you ask politely, most places will let you go through the stack to find a run that suits your needs. If you're looking at plain-sliced veneer, it is likely that the veneers will be quite wide. A quarter-sliced stack will most likely consist of narrower veneers. When considering which type of figure suits your piece,

consider also where the veneer joints will end up. This means you need to know your panel dimensions before you head out to the lumber dealer. A best-case scenario for a top panel might be a face-grain panel, where two book-matched veneers are wide enough to cover the entire top, with the seam dead center.

For the piece in this article, I used the top dimension as a rough guide because the sides were to be a bit narrower (due to the width of the corner post). I was able to line up the book-matched seam on the sides and the top. A second choice would have been to cover the top and the sides in four veneers (two book-matches). When neither of these is possible, I try to find a veneer that will cover the sides with one to run up one side, across the top, and down the other side.

Also essential to the furniture look are the corner posts—in this case 1 in. square. Make the side panels ⅞ in. thick, leaving a ⅛-in. shadow line on the outside and a flush surface on the inside. However, using solid posts with plywood panels creates a potential problem on the inside of the cabinet. Because the post is wider than the panel, a portion of it will be visible from inside, interrupting the smooth look of the maple interior. To correct this, I made the back post 1 in. wide but only ¼ in. thick and glued it into a shallow rabbet. The edge-banding on the back edge of the side panel completed this faux post (see the detail drawing on p. 76), allowing me to dado the back panel directly into the side panel for a seamless interior.

First, Make the Sandwiches

If your shop is big enough, lay out the sheets so that you can view them all at once. Examine each one and circle with a pencil anything that looks like a defect. Pay special attention to the ends, where the veneer seams are usually the worst. I try to avoid using the last few inches of a sheet. Measure the veneer widths and record any large changes that might fool you later. Determine whether the veneers run parallel to the edges. Most likely they won't, so plan on cutting them parallel before you crosscut.

The next step is to cut the face sheets and the cores. Because you'll be cutting oversized, there's no need to worry about tearout. I typically leave more on the length than on the width because crosscutting small amounts produces the worst tearout.

book-match and hope that a suitable cut will present itself for the top.

Plywood veneers may not be totally consistent in width. It's usually a small variation but something to watch out for nonetheless. In deciding how many sheets I need, I play it safe. An extra sheet gives me more options when it comes to laying out the cuts.

Hardwood plywood is one of the more expensive items at the lumberyard, and most places try to take good care of it, but dings and scratches are still possible. Commercial veneer is paper thin and easy to sand through. A good rule of thumb is if there is a scratch in it now, there will be a scratch in it forever. So I choose pieces carefully and then accept minor dings as character traits. When I

have found what I need, I ask for some of the 4x8 sheets of cardboard used for shipping to protect the material for the ride home and when storing it at my shop.

When picking out the interior stock, I'm not as particular. I like to use a light wood like maple. At all of the yards in my area, ¼-in.-thick maple is available only in rotary-sliced veneer, which means there will be no seams to worry about. Also, I take whichever core is available because small voids won't be noticed on the inside.

Some of the finest logs end up as plywood veneers. Most hardwood plywood dealers sell attractive sheet goods in a variety of common species, featuring rotary-sliced, book-matched, and quarter-sliced veneers.

CUTTING A PLYWOOD SHEET. A second sheet of plywood makes a serviceable edge guide for rough-cutting large sheets.

Create Custom Panels

Build up thicknesses by gluing ¼-in.-thick plywood sheets onto an MDF core. This technique puts the best faces of each sheet on display, allows the use of different species inside and outside the cabinet, and creates thicknesses greater than the standard ¾ in. This sandwich combines cherry and maple plywoods in a 1-in.-thick panel for the top of the cabinet.

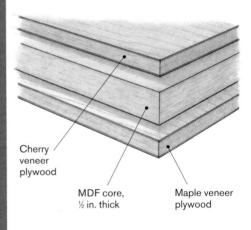

Cherry veneer plywood

MDF core, ½ in. thick

Maple veneer plywood

SPREAD GLUE EVENLY. Make a spreader by notching a thin piece of wood or plastic, which will regulate the amount of adhesive left behind. Only one surface needs glue. The pieces of blue tape keep everything in place during clamping.

CLAMPING CAULS APPLY EVEN PRESSURE. Edmundson's setup includes 4x4 timbers on the bottom of the sandwich and 2x3 cauls on top, which are sprung (tapered) about 1⁄16 in. on each end. He adds two sheets of melamine-coated particleboard above and below to help distribute the pressure. A couple of 2x4s below the setup create clearance for the clamp heads.

After you've made your oversized cuts in the sheet goods and cores, they are ready to be glued up. It's not as critical a procedure as it would be with thin veneers; the thickness of the plywood adds stiffness to the glue-up. I use a vacuum bag for clamping the plies, but I've had excellent results with clamps and sprung, or tapered, cauls, too. Yellow glue is fine as the adhesive.

After the carcase panels have been glued up, cut the sides to size. Wait to trim the top and bottom panels until you've glued the sides to the corner posts and have taken a final measurement.

RIPPING CUTS TEND TO BE CLEAN, but crosscuts are prone to tearout. Raise the blade well above the sheet and put the most important face up. Then wrap blue tape across the bottom and around the ends.

How to Avoid Tearout While Cutting Plywood

Even if your sawblade is sharp, it's difficult to saw commercial plywood without tearout. When veneer is sliced at the mill, it comes off the blade in a curve. This produces many tiny little splits on one side but leaves the other side smooth. If the veneers are book-matched, every other piece will be reversed and have the checks. These checked areas are especially prone to flaking and tearout on the table saw, especially when crosscutting.

Obviously, you want the important side of the panel facing up. However, you'll still find that the checked portions of book-matched veneers can flake off on the top. Raising the blade well above the work minimizes this but greatly increases tearout on the underside. Another problem spot is the end of a crosscut. If the cut isn't backed up, it can blow out. My solution to both problems is to run a strip of blue painter's tape where the kerf will be. Tape both under and on top of the plywood. After the cut, carefully peel away the tape from the sheet at a 90° angle. Of course, whenever possible, make crosscuts first and ripping cuts second to get rid of any blowout at the back edge. It's worth practicing these cutting tips on scrap.

Thin Edge-Banding Won't Be Noticed

Using the finished sides as a guide, measure and cut the top and bottom panels. After they have been cut to final size, apply the edge-banding. I don't like banding thicker than ⅜ in.; after that it stands out too much, at least to my eye. I leave it about 1/16 in. wider than the panel thickness and trim it flush after glue-up.

Attaching mitered edge-banding, especially on long pieces, takes practice and a little luck (see the sidebar on p. 74). It's difficult to line up the mitered ends exactly

Case Top: A Lesson in Edge-Banding

The edge-bandings on the top and bottom are mitered at their front edges for a better-looking corner. But they're not mitered at the back edges, which makes it much easier to apply the side edge-bandings.

APPLY EDGE-BANDING. Edmundson uses Bessey® K-Body clamps to hold everything square, and MDF cauls to distribute the pressure over the ⅜-in.-thick banding.

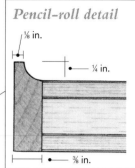

Pencil-roll detail

⅛ in.

¼ in.

⅜ in.

Pencil-roll profile

¼ in.

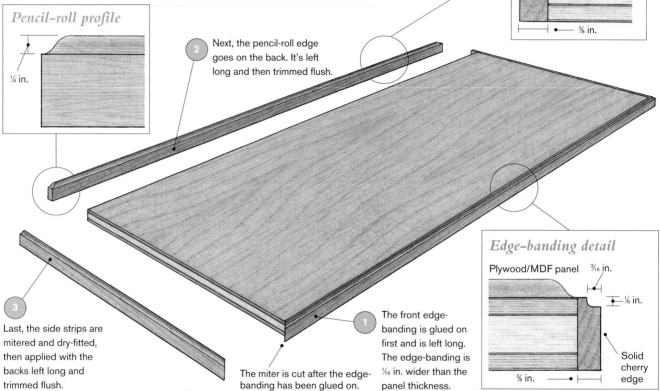

2 Next, the pencil-roll edge goes on the back. It's left long and then trimmed flush.

3 Last, the side strips are mitered and dry-fitted, then applied with the backs left long and trimmed flush.

1 The front edge-banding is glued on first and is left long. The edge-banding is ¹⁄₁₆ in. wider than the panel thickness.

The miter is cut after the edge-banding has been glued on.

Edge-banding detail

Plywood/MDF panel   ³⁄₁₆ in.

⅛ in.

⅜ in.

Solid cherry edge

PLANE AND SCRAPE THE EDGE-BANDING FLUSH. Don't go too far with the block plane before switching to a scraper. Use pencil squiggles to avoid the plywood.

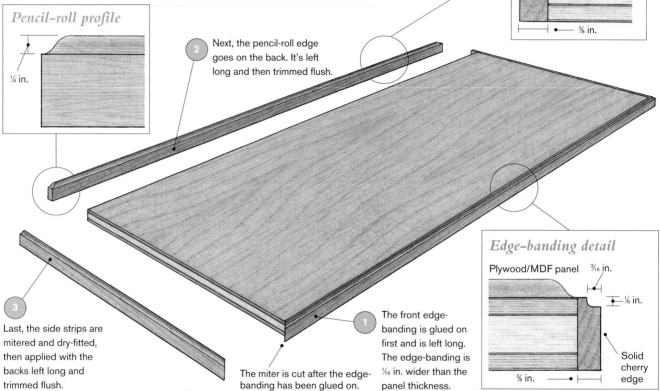

MITER THE FRONT EDGE-BANDING AFTER IT HAS BEEN APPLIED. This sounds counterintuitive, but it's easier to glue a long strip on this large panel when you don't have to line up precut miters perfectly. Lay out the cuts, saw close to the line (left), then clamp on a guide block for the final paring (right). Miter the side edge-banding to fit.

DETAIL THE PENCIL ROLL. The side edge-bandings are butted against the pencil roll at the back. Edmundson carves a gentle S-curve on the ends of the roll lip.

SAND THE PANELS. Before applying an edging that stands proud of the surface, sand the side and top panels. Go easy–it doesn't take long to sand through the thin veneer.

SEAL AND LEVEL THE SURFACE WITH SHELLAC. Pad on a 1-lb. cut of shellac, and then hand-sand with 320 grit. This prepares the thin veneers for a blotch-free oil finish.

with the corners of the panel. To increase your chances of success, leave the edge-banding long and cut the miters after glue-up. Mark the 45° miter with a pencil and cut slightly proud of the line with a pull saw. Next, use a try square to place a chopping block at the miter angle. You'll get better results from thinner paring cuts, so reposition the block a few times as you approach the line. Practice this technique on the bottom first, where small mistakes will be less obvious.

Before gluing on the side pieces, apply the banding at the back edges of the panels. On the top, apply a pencil roll. This oversized banding features a small cove that protrudes above the top to stop things from rolling off the back. The edge of the cove is flush with the top.

Mill the cove on thicker stock, then rip away the thin strip. Glue it on long just like the front edge. The closer you can get the cove flush to the top, the less work you'll have to do afterward. Use a wet rag to clean up glue squeeze-out; you want to minimize aggressive sanding on the plywood. There is no miter on the pencil roll, so run it long, then cut it flush with the panel edge after the glue has dried. Last, glue on the side

strips. These are mitered in front but left long in back and trimmed flush afterward.

Plane and scrape the edge-banding flush To trim edge-banding flush with the plywood surface, start with a handplane and scraper and finish up with the sander. (Flush-trimming router bits may do a fine job, but I'm a little leery of them.) Caution is the key to success. Don't get too close with the handplane, and be very careful with the sander. Use pencil squiggles along the edge to keep track of how much wood you're removing.

The pencil roll is harder to clean up without going through the thin veneer on the panel. If the glue-up went well, you won't have much to do. A profile sanding block or a curved scraper is a good thing to have. Again, use hash marks to keep track of where you're removing wood and where you're not.

Sand and Seal Flat Surfaces

Before attaching the corner posts, sand and seal the sides. The veneers will be pretty smooth right off the shelf. I usually start with 180 grit on my random-orbit sander, being careful to keep my hand moving

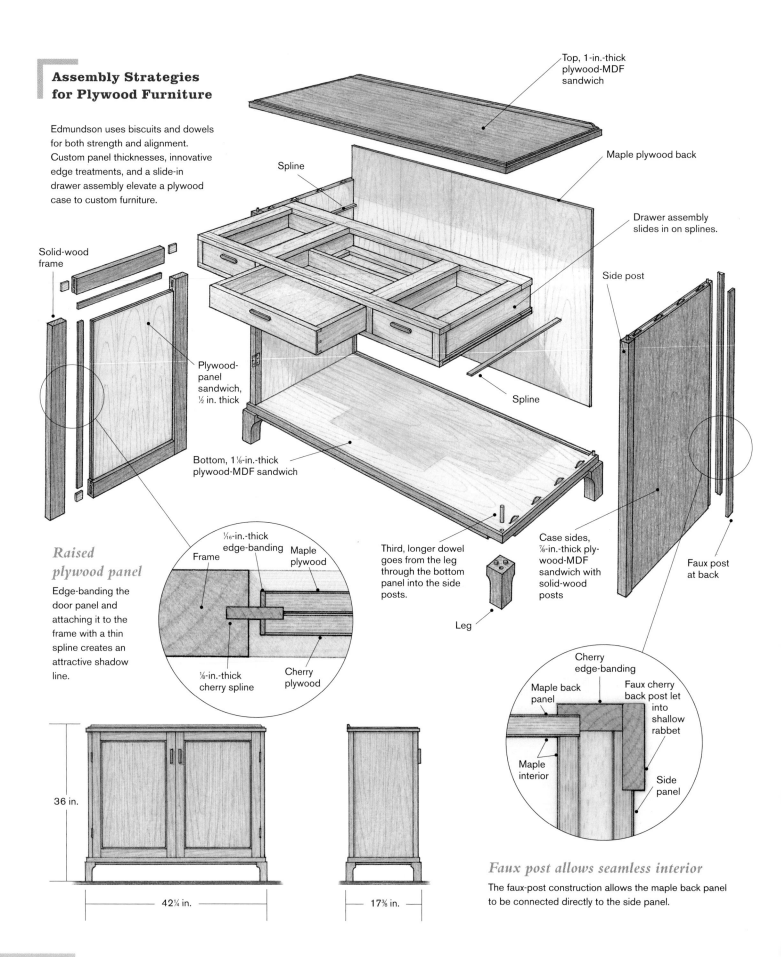

Assembly Strategies for Plywood Furniture

Edmundson uses biscuits and dowels for both strength and alignment. Custom panel thicknesses, innovative edge treatments, and a slide-in drawer assembly elevate a plywood case to custom furniture.

Top, 1-in.-thick plywood-MDF sandwich

Maple plywood back

Spline

Drawer assembly slides in on splines.

Side post

Solid-wood frame

Plywood-panel sandwich, ½ in. thick

Spline

Bottom, 1⅛-in.-thick plywood-MDF sandwich

Third, longer dowel goes from the leg through the bottom panel into the side posts.

Leg

Case sides, ⅞-in.-thick plywood-MDF sandwich with solid-wood posts

Faux post at back

Raised plywood panel

Edge-banding the door panel and attaching it to the frame with a thin spline creates an attractive shadow line.

Frame

¹⁄₁₆-in.-thick edge-banding

Maple plywood

⅛-in.-thick cherry spline

Cherry plywood

Cherry edge-banding

Maple back panel

Faux cherry back post let into shallow rabbet

Maple interior

Side panel

36 in.

42¼ in.

17⅜ in.

Faux post allows seamless interior

The faux-post construction allows the maple back panel to be connected directly to the side panel.

continuously over the piece. There will be no warning before you've sanded too much in one spot. Before you know it, you will see the glueline, and the panel will be ruined. If there is a scratch you think you can lessen, do so very lightly. Cabinet scrapers can be helpful, too, but never make more than a few passes. Do a test on that piece you practiced your crosscuts on to show yourself just how easy it is to burn through the veneer. After you've finished with 180 grit, be careful wiping off the dust. The small checks in the veneer tend to catch cloth fibers. I prefer to use a shop brush or vacuum to clean off the piece. Next, use 220 grit, clean off the dust, and then pad on a 1-lb. cut of shellac to fill the veneer. Last, sand with 320 grit using a sanding block. The shellac remains in the tiny checks and leaves a level surface.

Assembly of Plywood Furniture is Straightforward

Glue the front posts to the side panels using a simple butt joint, then apply the faux posts at the back edges and set the panels aside to work on the base.

The legs go on next. They fit into shallow recesses in the bottom panel, positioned for a ¼-in. reveal. Dowels are necessary to strengthen these applied feet. Use dowel locators to position two shallow pegs in the corners of the foot. Later, a third, longer dowel will be inserted from above, extending through the corners of the bottom panel and deep into the legs.

Cut stopped grooves in the top and bottom panels to accept the thin back panel. After dry-fitting the case sides to the bottom, use the groove in the bottom to line up the corresponding groove in the sides for a seamless fit.

The sides are attached to the bottom and top with biscuits and a dowel at each corner. I like a ⅛-in. reveal between the corner posts and the edges of the top and bottom. The biscuits strengthen the joint and align the pieces side to side. The dowels align the panels from front to back. As I said earlier, the dowels in the bottom corners are longer and extend down through the bottom panel and into the feet. After assembling the case, you can add a drawer box to the interior, as I did, and adjustable shelves.

DOWEL CENTERS ENSURE MATCHING HOLES.
Attach the legs to the bottom panel with two short dowels. Then drill a third hole through the bottom panel into the leg to accept a longer dowel that will extend up into the case side.

ATTACH THE TOP. Like the bottom, the top is located and attached with biscuits and dowels. The biscuits locate the panels side to side, and the dowels lock in the front-to-back alignment.

Dress Up the Doors with Visible Splines

Next, build and hang the doors. The door panels are glued up without an extra MDF core, so they end up ½ in. thick. To create a raised-panel variation, cut the glued panels approximately ⅜ in. smaller than the panel opening in the door. Glue on a ¹⁄₁₆-in.-thick solid edge, then cut a ⅛-in. slot into the panel and the door members. The panel is held in place by visible splines, creating a nice shadow line.

Finish with Sam Maloof's Recipe

After sanding and sealing the rest of the piece, apply the finish. I used Sam Maloof's 1:1:1 finish, made up of one part satin polyurethane, one part linseed oil, and one part tung oil. For the doors, I used mortised-in butt hinges and handmade handles. For adjustable shelves, I prefer brass pins with milled brass sleeves.

It's a shame not to utilize the wonderful veneers that end up on sheet goods. While the terms "commercial plywood" and "fine furniture" form an uncomfortable union for some purists, a little innovation yields a piece that truly feels custom. The key is using the strengths of commercial plywood to overcome its weaknesses.

MARK EDMUNDSON is a furniture maker in northern Idaho.

THE CHOICES FOR EDGING PLYWOOD
**vary in their complexity and durability
and in the time they take to execute.**

Six Ways to Edge Plywood

do about that ugly laminated edge. The goal is to create an edge treatment that looks like a continuation of the veneered surface without an obvious seam. You can achieve that goal with a simple layer of veneer or a more complex edge treatment that requires sophisticated joinery techniques.

The decision about how to treat a plywood edge can be influenced by a number of factors—aesthetic and design considerations (how do you want it to look?), function and durability (what kind of wear and tear will this edge face?), time and labor (how much of either do you want to spend?). The choice should depend on the planned use of the furniture piece or cabinet component. For example, a thick, solid edge would be appropriate for the exposed edge of a cabinet carcase. But for shelves contained and protected within a cabinet, an iron-on veneer edge would probably be sufficient. What follows is a look at the choices, from the easiest to apply but least durable to the more complicated versions that take longer but offer more protection.

BY MARIO RODRIGUEZ

T he choices vary in their complexity and durability and the time they take to execute.

To the world of woodworking, the innovation of plywood ranks right up there with the invention of the table saw. It's hard to imagine building some furniture and cabinetry without it. Plywood gives you the relative stability and flatness of a 4x8 panel, combined with the beauty of select veneers. You also get a variety of thicknesses, from ¼ in. to ¾ in. on stock items and up to 1½ in. on special orders—and you get all of this at a reasonable price. The challenge when using plywood is, of course, what to

MARIO RODRIGUEZ teaches woodworking in New York City and is a contributing editor to *Fine Woodworking*, as well as the author of several woodworking books.

Iron-On Veneer Is Easy to Apply

This material, also called edge tape or edge-banding, commonly measures $^{13}/_{16}$ in. wide for use with ¾-in.-thick plywood. It is sold in rolls from 8 ft. to 250 ft. long, and it is available in a number of different woods. Birch, cherry, mahogany, red oak, and walnut are fairly easy to find, but you can also buy it in ash, maple, pine, white oak, teak, and just about any other species of hardwood plywood that is made. Because it's so thin, edge-banding isn't suitable for furniture components that will be subject to heavy use. But once the heat-sensitive glue has melted and cooled and the edge-banding has been trimmed, the seams are virtually invisible. Just remember that heat causes the glue to release, so don't choose edge-banding for pieces that will be exposed to heat.

A standard household iron is the tool of choice for most people who use edge-banding. Set the iron to a medium heat level. While it's warming up, you can cut lengths of banding to size, allowing a little overhang on both ends. Move the iron slowly back and forth, applying a steady pressure until the heat-sensitive glue melts and bonds the edge-banding to the plywood. Some people burnish the banding with a scrap of wood, but I haven't found that technique necessary to get a good bond.

The glue needs to cool before you can trim the banding; otherwise, you end up with a gooey mess. You can trim the edge-banding overhang with a razor blade, a veneer saw, a file, or a specialty tool designed for the job.

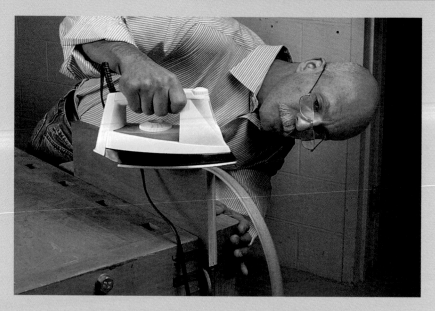

IRONING IS SIMPLE AND STRAIGHTFORWARD. A regular household iron set on medium heat is all you need to melt the heat-activated glue on the back of manufactured edge-banding. The material is available in just about any hardwood veneer that is also used to make plywood.

PLYWOOD GUIDES THE CUT. Rodriguez uses a sharp veneer saw to trim edge-banding on small workpieces that he can easily hold with one hand. To direct the cut, he keeps the bottom of the saw flat against the plywood.

THE RIGHT TOOL FOR THE JOB. For trimming large quantities of edge-banding, invest in a spring-loaded edge trimmer designed for this task. The one shown here is made by Virutex® and sells for about $10.

Solid Edging

With solid edging, you get a thicker edge than you do with iron-on edge-banding, and it requires only a little more work. For ¾-in.-thick plywood, begin by jointing a straight, square edge on a ⅞-in.-thick piece of solid lumber, then rip as many ⅛-in.-thick strips of lumber as you'll need.

I use a sharp 40-tooth rip blade, but a good alternate top bevel (ATB) blade can also do the job. Be sure to back up the cuts with a sturdy push stick to prevent the thin strips trapped between the spinning blade and the fence from shooting back at you. Before ripping each ⅛-in.-thick strip, joint the edge of the lumber. Place the jointed edge against the plywood edge when you glue it up.

After applying a swath of glue to the plywood edge, use a good-quality masking tape to clamp the edging strips in place. Inspect each edge after you tape it. A tight seam with a little bit of glue squeeze-out along the length of the joint indicates a good job. After the glue has dried, trim down the overhang with a block plane and a cabinet scraper.

MASKING TAPE MAKES A GOOD CLAMP. Numerous short pieces of masking tape provide plenty of pressure for gluing wood edging.

TOOLS FOR TRIMMING. Use a block plane to trim most of the excess edging flush to the plywood surface (above). Angle the sole of the plane to achieve a cleaner cut. A cabinet scraper finishes the job (right).

V-Shaped Edging Is Durable and Practically Seamless

This method offers a couple of important benefits. The V shape has an extremely low profile at the seam, making it nearly invisible; and the increased thickness toward the center offers more durability than you get with edge-banding or even the ⅛-in.-thick treatment.

Shape the solid-wood edging first, using a board wider than you need, which makes the process easier and safer. First, mark the exact center of the edging material with a marking gauge, then transfer that mark to the bottom edge of a sacrificial plywood fence. Set the table-saw blade to an angle of 25°, and set up the fence so that the spinning sawblade advances into the sacrificial fence just below the scribed line. Once this setup is ready, you can shape as many edgings as you need, beveling the top and bottom of each piece of lumber by flipping and turning each board around and passing it against the sawblade.

To cut the V shape into the edges of the plywood, leave the blade set at 25° and shift the fence to the other side of the blade. As with any finicky setup, it's best to have some scraps on hand to make adjustments as needed until the cut is aligned. When all of the angled cuts have been made, return the blade to 90° and rip the final pieces of V-molding from all of the lumber that you shaped. You can use masking tape to hold the V-molding in place when you glue it up. Once the glue sets, trim the edges with a block plane and a cabinet scraper.

THIS SETUP IS PRECISE. Transfer the lumber marking-gauge setting to a scrap of plywood. The scrap serves as a sacrificial fence for making the bevel cuts.

Cutting the Bevels

Use a ⅞-in.-thick piece of lumber to make a V-shaped edging for ¾-in.-thick plywood.

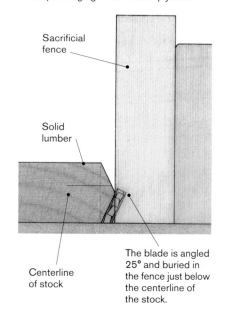

Sacrificial fence

Solid lumber

Centerline of stock

The blade is angled 25° and buried in the fence just below the centerline of the stock.

The goal is to create an edge treatment that looks like a continuation of the veneered surface without an obvious seam.

A NEARLY INVISIBLE SEAM AT THE EDGE. This alternative edging offers the advantage of showing very little wood at the edge where veneer meets lumber, unlike the effect you get with tongue-and-groove edges.

Shaping the Plywood

Move the fence to the other side of the blade to set up the cuts for the V shape into the edge of the plywood.

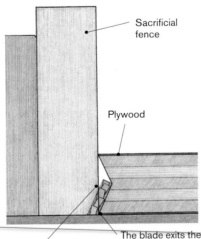

Sacrificial fence

Plywood

The blade angle and height remain unchanged.

The blade exits the fence just above the tabletop.

Three Tongue-and-Groove Edge Treatments

The three common versions of a tongue-and-groove lumber edge for plywood offer the most protection for a plywood edge. A significant advantage of adding a substantial piece of lumber to the edge of plywood is that you can shape that edge in any number of decorative configurations, such as a bullnose, an ogee, or a bevel.

But these edge treatments have a couple of drawbacks. They are time-consuming to carry out, and each of them produces a visibly discernible seam. You can go about cutting these joints a couple of different ways. You can buy a matched set of router bits to make the required cuts, or you can make all of the necessary cuts on a table saw using either a combination blade or a stacked dado set, or both. There's not a lot of room for mistakes when you're setting up these cuts—you must be precise.

I usually begin by plowing the grooves first, using a stacked dado set. Naturally, you must be prepared to make allowances for plywood that is not a full ¾ in. thick because it rarely is. Plowing the groove from both sides guarantees that it will be perfectly centered, regardless of the actual thickness. After plowing the grooves, clamp a plywood scrap to the fence and reposition it to cut the tongues to fit. I prefer to make the shoulder cuts first, using a combination blade for a clean cut. When gluing up any of the three versions shown here, a clamped, slightly concave batten will give you tighter seams, distribute the pressure more evenly across the span of the edge, and will require fewer clamps.

1 GROOVED PANEL
This version provides the most solid wood at the center, for shaping the edge later.

SHAPING LUMBER TONGUES ON THE TABLE SAW. Make the shoulder cuts first, with the edge stock flat on the table saw. Then turn the stock to a vertical position and run it through the blade again to cut the tongue to size.

START WITH LUMBER LARGER THAN NEEDED. When cutting joints in lumber edge stock, use wider boards and rip the edging down to width later, after shaping all of the joints.

TWO OPTIONS FOR PLOWING GROOVES. A stacked dado set or a straight-toothed rip blade each works well at cutting grooves into the edges of either plywood or solid lumber.

2 GROOVED LUMBER
This method is a little simpler to make but might limit the shapes you can mill into the edge.

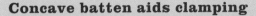

Concave batten aids clamping

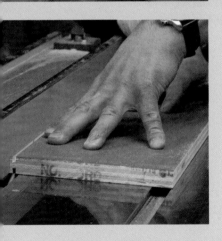

SAME PROCESS, BUT THE MATERIALS ARE REVERSED. A grooved lumber edge fitting over a plywood tongue is set up and cut just like its mirror-image cousin.

CUT THE SHOULDERS CAREFULLY. The quality of the joint where the plywood veneer meets the lumber edge is defined by how well the two materials come together. Maintain an even, steady cut for the best results.

3 PLYWOOD SPLINE
A separate spline serves as the tongue to join plywood to lumber.

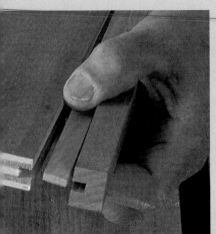

MATCHING GROOVES. This is the easiest and fastest of the three tongue-and-groove edge treatments to set up and cut. It reduces the joint-making time by half. Properly glued in place, the ¼-in.-thick plywood spline is plenty strong.

A CONCAVE BATTEN minimizes the number of clamps. A scrap of wood with a slight bow in it (above) requires fewer clamps to get even pressure along an edge being glued up. A block plane (left) makes quick work of leveling the solid wood.

Frame-and-Panel Doors: An Illustrated Guide

BY
GRAHAM BLACKBURN

Whatever else is required, design in a style that is in harmony with other woodwork in the room.

Before the advent of frame-and-panel construction, doors (and their owners) were at the mercy of wood movement. Solid plank doors were unruly—likely to split, warp, and twist. Subject to expansion and contraction across their entire width, they'd gape open when the weather was dry and swell shut when it was wet. Frame and panel changed all that. Instead of ignoring or resisting wood movement, frame and panel was designed to accommodate it.

Frame and panel soon became one of the indispensible building blocks of work in solid wood, used not just in doors but in all sorts of case construction and paneling. Over the centuries, the range of its applications has been equalled only by the diversity of stylistic treatments it has received.

Given all this variety, where does a woodworker start when designing frame-and-panel doors? With the structure. It is my feeling that before you can make something look good, you have to be able to make it work well. Once you understand why and how frame and panel works, you are halfway to a successful design. In the drawings on the following pages, I've laid out the underpinnings of frame-and-panel construction and followed them with a selection of considerations that inform the design process.

The Structural Nitty-Gritty

The simple genius of the frame-and-panel system is in making a dimensionally stable frame of narrow members and allowing a large solid panel to expand and contract freely inside it. The panel may be large or small, plain or simple, but as long as it is made of solid wood it must be free to move (so that it will not split or buckle with changes in humidity) and at the same time be securely held (so that it cannot warp). Panels are typically held by their edges in grooves formed in the surrounding frame, and they are pinned or glued only at the center. Occasionally, the grooves are formed by adding a strip of molding to a rabbet, but most often the groove is integral.

The frame members are most commonly mortised and tenoned together, although other methods such as plate joinery or doweling can be used. Because most panels are oriented with their grain running vertically, the rails have the most work to do in preventing the panel from warping. Therefore, the rails are usually the widest parts of the frame. So the frame does not appear top-heavy, the top rail is often made a little narrower than the bottom rail. The stiles are generally made narrower still, giving a pleasing appearance and minimizing the seasonal change in the width of the door.

86 DOORS

The proportions of the frame joints may vary depending on the size and function of the piece: More substantial doors should be joined with tenons approximating one-third of the thickness of the members; joints for lighter doors may be a quarter of the thickness.

Purposeful Design

Working up the proportions of a door's parts from a structural standpoint will go a long way to producing a pleasing design. But without compromising structural integrity, there remains much you can do to control the final appearance.

You can change the apparent shape of any door by altering the size, shape, and number of framing members and reinforce the message with compatible grain patterns. To make an extremely vertical door appear less tall and narrow, for example, try using multiple rails and orienting the grain of the panels horizontally, or make a square door stretch vertically by giving it a number of tall, narrow panels. If you are designing a long, low piece and are concerned it will appear squat and heavy, you can give the piece more lift by dividing the doors so the top panels are smaller than the lower ones.

Control of the focus is another useful design tool. To avoid visual confusion, pick out certain elements of the design for emphasis. For example, you might use plain panels in an unusual frame or surround a strikingly grained panel with a straight-grained frame.

Whatever else is required, design in a style that is in harmony with other woodwork in the room. Even if you don't design in the exact style of the surroundings, try to include elements that will relate, such as elegantly raised panels in a piece destined for a roomful of Colonial furniture or flat panels for a piece that will live with Arts and Crafts furniture.

GRAHAM BLACKBURN is a furniture maker, illustrator, and author who lives in Woodstock, New York.

ENTRY DOOR

QUEEN ANNE CUPBOARD

ARTS AND CRAFTS SIDEBOARD

Construction:
Frame-and-Panel Doors

What's the point of frame and panel?

Solid plank doors are at the mercy of seasonal changes in humidity. Hence, they are unlikely to fit their openings in both summer and winter. Frame and panel solved the problem, making a stable frame and allowing a solid panel to expand and contract inside it.

PLANK-AND-BATTEN DOOR
IGNORES WOOD MOVEMENT

FRAME-AND-PANEL DOOR
ACCOMMODATES WOOD MOVEMENT

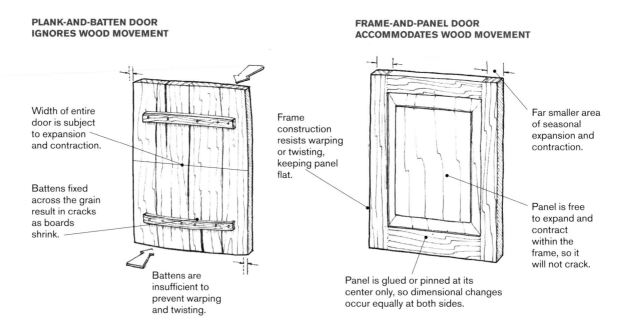

Width of entire door is subject to expansion and contraction.

Battens fixed across the grain result in cracks as boards shrink.

Battens are insufficient to prevent warping and twisting.

Frame construction resists warping or twisting, keeping panel flat.

Far smaller area of seasonal expansion and contraction.

Panel is free to expand and contract within the frame, so it will not crack.

Panel is glued or pinned at its center only, so dimensional changes occur equally at both sides.

Basic structure of a frame-and-panel door

In a typical frame-and-panel door, the stiles run through from top to bottom, and the grain in the panels is vertical. The rails are generally wider than the stiles, providing wider tenons and better resistance to warping of the panels. One rough rule of thumb suggests that if the bottom rail is one unit wide, the top rail should be two-thirds of a unit wide and the stiles one-half of a unit wide.

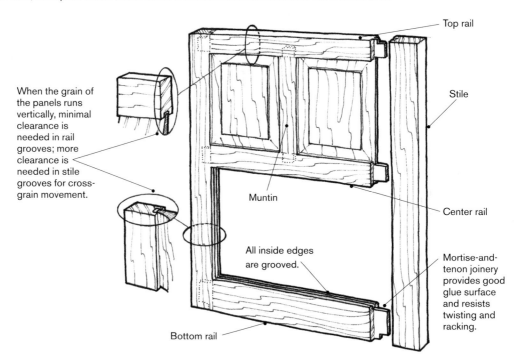

When the grain of the panels runs vertically, minimal clearance is needed in rail grooves; more clearance is needed in stile grooves for cross-grain movement.

Top rail

Stile

Muntin

Center rail

All inside edges are grooved.

Mortise-and-tenon joinery provides good glue surface and resists twisting and racking.

Bottom rail

Joinery options

THREE WAYS TO JOIN THE FRAME

Lighter cabinet doors, especially those with glued-in plywood panels, may be joined with biscuits or dowels.

Mortise and tenon is strongest. The haunch of the tenon increases the joint's resistance to twist.

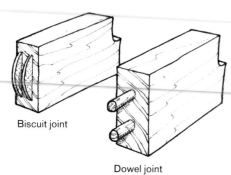

Biscuit joint

Dowel joint

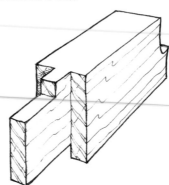

Mortise and haunched tenon

JOINERY LAYOUT

Cutting the panel grooves in line with the mortises and tenons makes layout and execution easier.

Haunch fills through-groove.

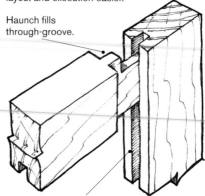

Panel groove runs through.

PANEL-HOLDING OPTIONS

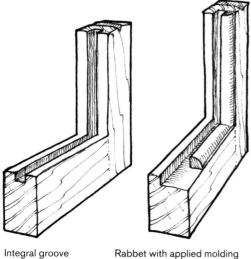

Integral groove

Rabbet with applied molding

Applied bolection molding supplies strength without using much space in the rabbet.

Applied bolection molding

Face-mounting panels is useful when frame members are too narrow to groove or rabbet.

Plywood panel

Face-mounted panel

COPE AND STICK

An edge that is profiled is said to have a "stuck" molding. The corresponding contour is "coped."

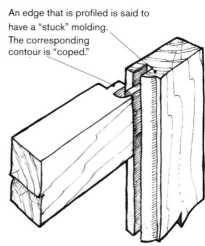

Note: On small cabinet doors, a tongue on the rail instead of a full tenon suffices for joinery.

PANEL VARIATIONS

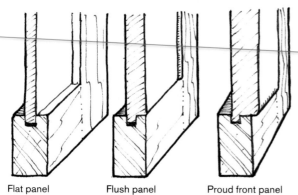

Flat panel

Flush panel

Proud front panel

A fielded panel is one with a defined center section: the field. For cabinet work, panels are generally flat on the inside face.

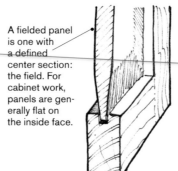

Fielded panel

Although the term is often used more broadly, a raised panel is one in which the center, or field, is defined by a shoulder.

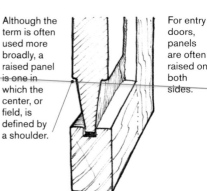

For entry doors, panels are often raised on both sides.

Fielded and raised panel

Design:
Frame-and-Panel Doors

Working within a given space

DESIGNS FOR A SQUARE OPENING

Different effects can be achieved for similar spaces by changing the visual focus.

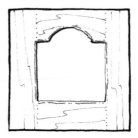

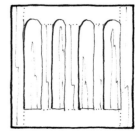

Focus on the framing: Concentrate the shaping on the frame members, and keep the panel neutral in color and pattern.

Focus on the panel: Use dramatic grain matching or veneer within a plain frame.

Stretch the square: Downplay the squareness of the opening by designing a door with strong vertical elements.

DESIGNS FOR A VERTICAL OPENING

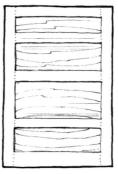

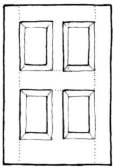

Restate the shape: Keeping the design as simple as possible preserves the essential shape of the opening.

Accentuate the lateral: Introducing strong horizontal elements—three center rails, wide panels with strong grain running side to side—offsets the door's verticality.

Beefing up the rectangle: Raised panels make a door look stronger and heavier; a traditional four-square approach with slightly taller bottom panels provides good balance in a rectangular opening.

MULTIPLE DOORS FOR A HORIZONTAL SPACE

Stiles at either end of cabinet are made double-wide to balance the paired stiles between. Placing the center rail above the mid-point creates tall lower panels, which give the long, low cabinet a vertical emphasis. For visual balance, the top rail plus the cabinet top equal the width of the bottom rail.

Center rail   Narrow stile   Wide stile

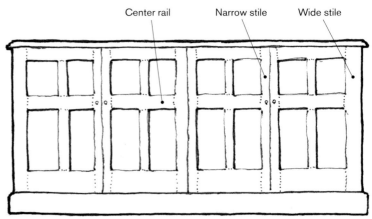

Designing with period styles

Use the characteristics of a period style to design a door in harmony with its surroundings.

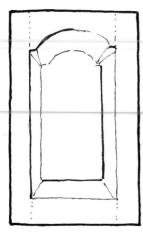

18th century: Classic proportions, raised panels; made of mahogany.

Contemporary: Geometric proportions, unadorned forms; contrasting materials.

Victorian Gothic: Emphasis on verticality, pointed arch panels, linen-fold carving; polychrome finish or walnut or fumed oak.

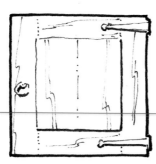
Arts and Crafts: Bold, simple forms, minimal molding, wrought-iron hardware; made of oak.

Proportioning by the book

Although the designer's eye should always be the final judge of what looks good, there are a number of traditional systems you can use to establish pleasing proportions.

USING THE GOLDEN MEAN

The golden mean may be expressed as a ratio, BC:AB as AB:AC. This is approximately 5:8.

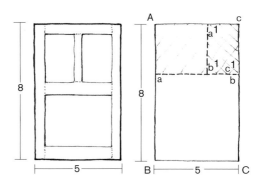

ABCc is a golden rectangle. Squaring a golden rectangle leaves another golden rectangle (shaded area Aabc); squaring this rectangle produces yet another golden rectangle (double-shaded area a1b1c1c). This smallest rectangle produced the shape of the door's upper panels.

USING THE CLASSICAL ORDERS OF ARCHITECTURE

The Tuscan column (the first of the five classical orders of architecture) is built on a ratio of 1:7. The column width = 1, the column height = 7. All other dimensions are multiples or fractions of this ratio; for example, the base and the capital are each one-half the column width.

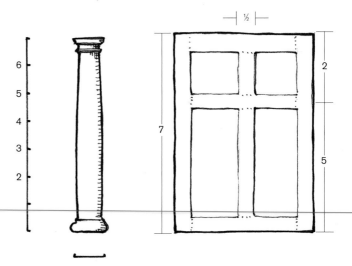

Use the ratio of the Tuscan order (or any other order) to proportion a door. Divide the height of the door by seven, then use multiples or fractions of the resulting unit to size the panels and frame members. (For an 84-in. door, the unit would be 12 in.)

Three Ways to Make Cabinet Doors

BY STEVE LATTA

I n a perfect world, all cabinet doors would be constructed using stout mortise-and-tenon joints, built to last generations. When I reproduce an 18th-century piece, I build doors whose joints will outlast these achy joints of mine. My clients pay for that, and I would not sleep at night giving them anything less.

At the other end of the spectrum, would I go to the same effort for a bathroom vanity that will end up on the curb after the next remodel? Probably not. There are faster ways to make a door. A door meant for hiding everything from towels to toilet cleansers doesn't have to rise to the level of a hutch.

I could come up with a dozen or more methods to join doors, but there are three that will solve most needs: doors for the finest furniture, doors for glass panels, and low-budget doors that you need to get done in a hurry.

Solid Panel

FULL MORTISE-AND-TENON JOINTS make this the best method for constructing fine furniture. Additionally, the tenon's offset shoulder adds rigidity to the joint. The profiled corner must be mitered for the joint to close.

Best Method for Strong, Classic Frames

After cutting the stock to its rough size, mold a profile and cut a slot in all of the frame members. Although sometimes I'll use just the sticking portion of a cope-and-stick set to cut the profile and groove in one pass, I often resort to standard router bits. By mixing and matching standard bits, I have an infinite variety of profiles available to me. Cope-and-stick bits come in just a handful of profiles. To cut the slot, you can use a slot-cutting bit or a dado head on the table saw.

Mortises are cut next. These are usually located on the stile members. Cut them with your preferred tool, the same thickness as the width of the groove, flush with the walls of the groove. I generally cut the mortises to within ⅜ in. of the outside edges of the doors. But if you're making doors whose backs will be rabbeted for an overlay construction, leave at least ⅜ in. beyond the mortise. That way, when you cut the rabbet

Glass Panel

THERE'S NO OFFSET SHOUL-
DER on the tenon in this joint
because an offset shoulder
would get in the way of the
rabbet for the glass panel.
Nonetheless, the frame, built
with full mortise-and-tenon
joints, is very solid.

Cope-and-Stick

COPE-AND-STICK BITS are
used to machine the profile,
groove, and stub tenons. To
strengthen the weak stub
tenon, glue a plywood panel
in the frame.

Frames for Solid-Wood Panels

SHAPE THE RAILS AND STILES ON THE
ROUTER TABLE. The sticking portion of a
cope-and-stick bit cuts the profile and
groove in one pass. Set the fence flush
with the bearing.

RAILS MUST HAVE OFFSET SHOULDERS.
Guide the stock along the table saw fence
and push it using a backer block for extra
support.

CUTTING THE CHEEKS WITHOUT A
TENONING JIG. The rail is pushed along
an auxiliary fence clamped to the table
saw's fence. A backer block prevents
tearout.

around the perimeter of the door frame, you won't cut into the joint.

Next, cut tenons on the rails. This involves a couple of setups on the table saw because the rear shoulder is offset more than the front shoulder. The offset has two advantages: It adds an element of triangulation to the joint, which makes it very strong, and it looks good from both sides. Begin by cutting the shoulders on the table saw, which will require two setups. Then cut the cheeks. To account for shrinkage, I prefer to machine tenons a hair oversized, then let the stock settle overnight.

For a tight fit, handplane the cheeks until the joint slips together snugly. Lastly, the molded profile must be mitered at the inside corners. I do this by hand, using a chisel and a simple jig. To locate the miter, fit a rail to a stile as far as it will go, mark the inside corner, disassemble, and clamp the jig to the stock. Then shave away the waste with a chisel.

This method produces an exceptional joint that can be improved by draw-boring or wedging either a blind or through-tenon. With a typical 1½-in.-long tenon, the amount of glue surface is about four times that of a ⅜-in. stub tenon, the kind you typically end up with when using cope-and-stick router bits. It's unlikely that you'll ever have to repair a door built this way.

Door Frames for Glass Panels and More

When a project calls for doors with glass panels, you need a frame with a rabbet on the back to house the glass. Although you could use the previous method for glass-paneled doors, it's not ideal. Because of the offset shoulder cut on the rails, a rabbet cut into the back of the frame will also end up offset and won't look good.

After milling the rail and stile stock to rough sizes, I run the molding. Cut the profile using either of the previous methods: by using the sticking portion of a cope-and-stick bit or by mixing and matching standard router bits.

Next, cut the mortises, same as before. The tenons, however, are cut differently. Forget about setting up for the extra shoulder cut on the back of the rails. Cut all of the tenons with continuous shoulders all the way around. Again, make them a hair thick and let them sit overnight.

MAKE FINAL ADJUSTMENTS USING A CHISEL. The back wall of the groove on the stiles must be removed up to the miter. On both rails and stiles, use a guide block–a piece of scrap cut at 45° and clamped to the stock–to miter the inside corners of the profile.

Frames for Glass Panels

USE A STICKING BIT OR MAKE YOUR OWN PROFILE FROM STOCK ROUTER BITS. A straight bit, left, a cove bit, and a slot cutter were used to mold this profile. As an added touch, both sides of this frame were profiled.

SHOULDERS ARE THE SAME HEIGHT ON ALL SIDES OF THE RAILS. After cutting the shoulders, raise the blade high enough to remove the cheeks.

MITER BOTH WALLS OF THE GROOVE. Using a guide block and chisel, pare away the miter, which in this construction will show on both the front and back of the door.

A GLASS PANEL IS FITTED FROM THE REAR. After ripping away the rear wall of the groove, insert the glass and secure it with small strips of wood nailed or screwed in place.

SAME METHOD, TWO APPLICATIONS. By profiling both walls of the slot (top), you can make an elegant frame for a solid panel. Or rip off the rear wall (bottom) and fit a glass panel.

Fast Frames for Plywood Panels

COPE-AND-STICK BITS DO MOST OF THE WORK. The sticking portion of the bit cuts the profile and groove in one pass. These bits are best suited for ¾-in.- to ⅞-in.-thick stock.

As in the previous method, the molded profile must be mitered for the joint to close. But because there's not an offset on the shoulders of the rails, both the front (the profiled edge) and rear walls of the slots must join in a miter. Use the same jig as mentioned earlier and a wide chisel to miter both walls at the same time. When you dry-fit the frame, you'll notice the back looks funny because of the miter. But for glass panels, rip off the rear walls of the groove, which eliminates the miter. To hold the glass, I'll often rely on tinted glazing putty alone. You could also rip strips of the same species of wood and screw or nail them in place, mitered at the corners. (Cut the bottom piece in two for ease of removal should the glass need replacement.)

If you like this construction method (it's faster than the first) and want to apply it to floating wood panels, here's a trick to make the back of the frame look as elegant as the front. Run a profile along the back inside edge of the frame. That funny-looking miter is transformed into an elegant inside corner, and the door will look good on both sides.

Cope-and-Stick Joints Need Reinforcement

A lot of inexpensive kitchen cabinets are built using cope-and-stick router bits. These tools cut the profile, groove, and stub tenons in two quick operations. Many of these bits leave you with ⅜-in.-long tenons. (For more on the styles of cope-and-stick bits, see the sidebar on p. 98.) Some router-bit manufacturers, such as Jesada®, offer bits that cut ⁷⁄₁₆-in.-long tenons. That's a slight

ROUT THE MATCHING COPING. Use a backer block when cutting the coping along the end grain of the rails.

WHERE COPE-AND-STICK JOINTS FAIL. The molded edge, which has been reduced in thickness, is a weak spot in this joint. That's why it's a good idea to glue plywood panels into the grooves of the door frame, which will produce a much sturdier door overall.

improvement, but I wouldn't put solid-wood floating panels in door frames joined this way. A combination of seasonal movement and an occasional slammed door will take a toll.

The weak point of cope-and-stick doors is the profiled edge. Routing the profile removes a fair amount of wood. Yet this area is expected to do double duty as a mortise wall. Pull or push too hard on a door, and the stub tenon will split off the molded edge. The stub-tenon-to-groove glue joint is another weak area. There's not a lot of surface area to glue, and if you mill these parts a little loose or the wood shrinks, the joint will fail.

To strengthen these joints, use a plywood panel (or other manmade product) and glue it on all four sides to the grooves. I know some woodworkers who try to beef up the stub tenons with dowels or loose tenons and then install floating solid-wood panels. They can help, but I've seen these fail prematurely. On most pieces of furniture, we're not talking about a lot of joints. Making full mortise-and-tenon joints just makes sense to me.

STEVE LATTA is an instructor at the Thaddeus Stevens Institute of Technology in Lancaster, Pennsylvania.

Cope-and-Stick Router Bits

There are three types of cope-and-stick (sometimes called rail-and-stile) router bits: reversible, combination, and matched. All must be used in a router table. And although each bit has a bearing mounted on its shaft, I always use a router fence set flush with the bearing for extra support. To understand these bits, it helps to define their components.

The sticking is the profile and groove that is cut along the edge (long grain) of the stile and rail. The coping is the reverse pattern that is cut on the end (end grain) of the rail. The coping cutter leaves a stub tenon as deep as the groove for the panel. For a tight-fitting joint, the bits must be machined to high tolerances, and this isn't always the case. If you can't get a joint to fit after much trial and error, contact the manufacturer and see about getting a replacement. All of these bits require set-up time. Once you have a setup that produces good joints, make samples and keep them for reference.

Although prices vary greatly among manufacturers, reversible bits tend to be the least expensive of the three types. They're also the most difficult to use. After routing the sticking, a locknut must be removed in order to flip-flop the top cutter before machining the coping. Shims may have to be

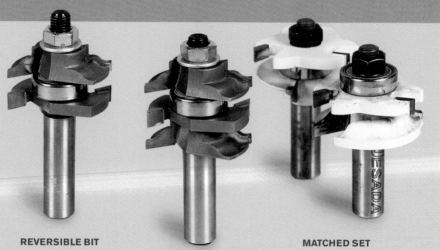

REVERSIBLE BIT

COMBINATION BIT

MATCHED SET

fitted between the bearing and top cutter to fine-tune the fit.

Combination bits, which are intermediately priced, have all three cutters positioned on the bit's shaft. To change between the coping and sticking cuts, the bit is either raised or lowered. Again, shimming may be necessary to get a good fit. With some bits, it's just hard to get a good fit; either the tenon is snug and the coping is loose, or vice versa.

The most expensive option is to purchase a set of matched bits that are machined to complement each other. Although I've never conducted an in-depth comparison test, among a random sampling of bits I had on hand, the matched set produced the best fit.

REVERSIBLE BITS ARE ADJUSTED BY USING SHIMS. A good-fitting coping and snug-fitting stub tenon require some trial-and-error when adjusting the distance between the cutters.

Quick but Sturdy Cabinet Door

QUIRK-AND-BEAD MOLDING AND AN ANTIQUED STAIN AND LACQUER FINISH give Mario Rodriguez's pine, plywood-paneled door an air of simple period elegance.

BY MARIO RODRIGUEZ

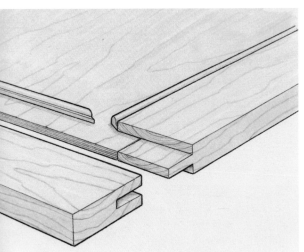

When I had to make a batch of pantry cabinets in a hurry and at a low cost, I developed the design for this frame-and-panel door. I wanted the door to have a traditional flavor and reasonable strength but obtained with the least possible labor and materials. I decided to use a plywood panel and dress it up with a simple quirk-and-bead molding. I planned the simplest joinery I could, and then I decided to apply the molding instead of milling it onto the frame pieces. The molding is easily made with a stock router bit, and the quirk, or recess, behind the bead produces a dramatic shadow that gives the flat-paneled door its visual weight. The design is well-suited for small- or medium-sized doors on kitchen cabinets, vanities, and built-in storage units and will look as good painted as with a clear finish.

Grooving Non-Stop

I chose ¼-in. plywood (good on both sides) for the panel to keep the door light and stock preparation to a minimum. Frame-and-panel construction accommodates the expansion and contraction of a solid panel by allowing it to float in the frame. Here, with no wood movement to worry about, I was able to glue the panel on all four sides, making it a structural element of the door. I greatly simplified the joinery by housing both the panel and the rail tenons in the same ¾-in.-deep groove (see the drawing on p. 99). At ¾ in., the tenons are somewhat short, but the plywood panel glued all the way around at full depth in the groove adds considerably to the door's strength.

This technique not only removes the need for making separate mortises for the tenons but also means that you don't have to stop the grooves on the stiles as you normally would with frame-and-panel doors. Instead, you just run the grooves the full length of all the frame members.

I usually plane my frame stock ¾ in. thick and rip the pieces 2 in. wide. Then I groove the inside edge of each piece on the table saw. Because ¼-in. plywood is usually somewhat less than ¼ in. thick, I don't bother with dado blades. I just cut the groove in two passes with a regular blade raised to ¾ in. However you cut the groove, it will be helpful to mill extra stock with the frame members for use as test pieces as you seek the setting that will give the panel a snug fit.

Rails Get Tenons

Next, I cut the cheeks of the tenons. Because the tenon length is the same as the groove depth, I leave the table saw's blade at the same height I used to cut the groove. I mount the rails onto a simple, shopmade jig for safety and support (see the photo below).

I cut the tenon shoulders on the table saw using the miter gauge. I use the fence as an end stop, which is permissible here (though it isn't in normal crosscutting). That's because I'm not cutting all the way through the piece, so there's no danger of kickback or jamming. You could also use a stop block clamped to an extended fence on your miter gauge.

Size Up the Panel

I use ¼-in. cabinet-grade plywood for the panels in most doors like these. For larger or heavier-duty doors, it would be advisable to split the panel with a medial rail or use ½-in. plywood and rabbet around the back to produce a ¼-in. tongue.

When I cut out the panels, I take particular care to ensure that they come out square. Then, when I glue up the frame members around them, I can rely on the panel to make the door square and the glue-up trouble-free.

TENONING JIG FROM SCRAP. A stick of pine nailed to a square of medium-density fiberboard makes a jig to produce reliable tenons.

KERF BETWEEN THE BEADS
TO CUT THEIR BACK EDGE,
**and then rip the two pieces
from the board.**

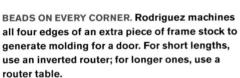

**BEADS ON EVERY CORNER. Rodriguez machines
all four edges of an extra piece of frame stock to
generate molding for a door. For short lengths,
use an inverted router; for longer ones, use a
router table.**

Attending to Assembly

When I assemble the doors, I apply glue
generously in the grooves and on the
tenons. Then I lightly clamp the rails and
stiles around the panels. Next, I double-
check for squareness and clean up the glue
squeeze-out. After removing the clamps, I
clean up the frame and fair the joints with a
sharp block plane.

Quirky Molding

The quirk-and-bead molding can be
produced from excess frame stock with a
beading cutter in a router. I bead all four
corners of the stock on a router table or
simply a router upside down with a fence
clamped to the base, as shown in the photo
above. To free the pieces of molding, I cut a
kerf down the middle of each edge (see the
top photo at right) and then rip through
the full thickness of the stock.

I cut the miters for the molding on the
table saw with the miter gauge, but the
miters can be cut nearly as fast with a dove-

**MASKING TAPE SUPPLIES ALL
THE CLAMPING PRESSURE
you need to glue up the molding. The shadow line created
by the quirk behind the bead
gives a bit of leeway in correcting small mitering errors.**

tail saw and a block plane for fitting. First, I
dry-assemble the molding. Then I glue it in
with yellow glue and hold it in place with
masking tape, as shown in the photo above.
I close minor misalignments at the miters
by pulling the molding away from the
frame slightly. The tiny gap created behind
the molding won't be noticed—it will read
as part of the shadow that gives this simple
molding its distinction.

MARIO RODRIGUEZ teaches woodworking in
New York City and is a contributing editor to *Fine
Woodworking*, as well as the author of several wood-
working books.

Fitting Flush-Mounted Doors

BY STEVEN THOMAS BUNN

Installing flush-mounted doors is the bane of many woodworkers. The trick is putting them in so they fit with even gaps all around and so they lie smoothly in plane with the case front. I've fitted hundreds of doors for Thomas Moser's cabinet shop. Over the years, I've learned some tricks for installing doors accurately without a lot of measuring. If, after following this step-by-step guide, your doors still aren't exactly right, the sidebar on pp. 106–107 has some tips on how to make the adjustments.

WELL-FITTED DOORS SHOW QUALITY CRAFTSMANSHIP. Inset doors that fit with tight even gaps are a sign of quality work. An organized approach simplifies the process and helps eliminate sloppily hung doors.

Make Doors Oversized

A crucial step to properly fitting doors is to make them slightly oversized in both height and width. I make my doors ⅛ in. to ¾₆ in. larger than their openings, so I have plenty of material to trim to a precise fit.

Fitting the Doors

When you fit doors and install hinges, always work on a level, flat surface. Every time you move the piece, it racks the carcase, which can affect the door opening. When the completed piece is installed, I use small, tapered wedges under the corners as necessary to return the carcase to a level position and correct any misalignment in the doors.

My goal when fitting doors is to have a ¾₆-in. gap at the bottom and sides and ½₂ in. to ¾₆ in. at the top. For double doors, I shoot for the same gaps at sides, top, and bottom and ¾₂ in. to ⅛ in. between the doors (see the photo at right) to allow for expansion and opening clearance. You can use these same techniques, however, to create whatever gap suits you.

The first step is to determine the width of the opening. I measure at the top, middle, and bottom and use the largest dimension to calculate the trimmed width of my doors. I make a single door ¾₆ in. narrower than the largest opening dimension, which leaves another ¾₆ in. for final trimming. If double doors are to go in the opening, I subtract ¾₆ in. from the largest dimension and divide by two to get the width for each door. This leaves ¾₆ in. for opening the center gap to final width after the doors are hung.

I rip the doors to width, being careful to take equal amounts off each stile. If one stile is more than ½₂ in. wider than the other, it will probably be obvious after assembly. I make a light jointer pass on each edge to clean up the sawmarks.

I set the doors in the opening and push them tightly against the hinge stiles to

CUTTING DOORS DOWN TO SIZE. A sliding-crosscut box for the table saw makes it easy to trim doors accurately to size. A paper shim between the fence and the door produces a tapered bottom rail to fit an out-of-square opening.

check the fit. Then I joint equal amounts off both doors as necessary to create a ¾₆ in. overall center gap. The door isn't trimmed to height until later in the fitting process.

Fitting the hinge stile and bottom To establish a known starting point for fitting the door, I trim the bottom rail square to the hinge stile using a sliding-crosscut box on my table saw. Next I set the first door in the case opening with the bottom rail resting flat on the bottom face-frame member and push the door gently against the case side. If the case is truly square, the hinge rail will rest flat against the case side, and I go on to fit the top of the door. In my experience, this is rare. Case panel sides can be out of square or slightly trapezoidal because of faulty glue-up or because the case bottom is larger or smaller than the top. The result is the door touches the case side at the top or the bottom with a gap at the opposite end. Most of the gaps that I have encountered range from as narrow as a piece of paper to as large as $\frac{1}{16}$ in.

To eliminate the gap between the hinge stile and the case side and to get the door to fit the out-of-square opening, I cut the door's bottom rail at an angle. I use the same crosscut box on my table saw, but this time, I shim out either the top or bottom of the hinge stile with folded paper or a wedge to taper the bottom rail, as shown in the photo on p. 103. I made a rough approximation of the shim's thickness by butting the door's hinge stile gently against the case side and measuring the gap, either at the top or bottom, between the door and the carcase. I find it helpful to mark the corner that needs to be shimmed, so I don't get confused when placing the door in the crosscut box. I take as small a cut as possible and test-fit the door after each cut. After fitting the door's bottom and hinge sides, I clean up the bottom edge on the jointer, taking off no more than $\frac{1}{32}$ in.

Fitting the top To fit the top of the door, I place it back in its opening, resting the door bottom on two pennies. The pennies act as $\frac{1}{16}$-in. spacers. Holding the door in the opening so the back of the door is tight against the face frame at the top of the opening, I strike a pencil line across the inside of the top of the door, as shown in the photo below. This line determines both the angle that must be cut on the top rail and the door's length. I then measure down and draw a second line parallel to and $\frac{1}{32}$ in. below the initial line. Cutting to the top line allows the door to drop into the opening.

ACCURATE LAYOUTS WITHOUT MEASURING. **Marking the door in place is more accurate than transferring measurements. Penny-spacers under the bottom rail establish the bottom gap.**

Cutting to the lower line establishes a $\frac{1}{32}$-in. door gap. Again, as with the bottom rail, I use shims and make multiple passes with the crosscut box on the table saw to establish the correct angle and work down to the line, adjusting my shims in or out as necessary to split the line with the sawblade.

Be patient: Taking off too much too soon may leave you with a badly fitting top rail or a door too short to be of use. Don't cut to the second and final pencil line until you are satisfied with the cut of the first. Checking the door as soon as it will drop into the opening gives me a second chance to verify that my pencil guidelines were correct. Cutting directly to the second line without test-fitting can result in a lopsided fit. The error may be less than $\frac{1}{64}$ in., but the eye catches small differences in the gap between one side and the other of the door and case and magnifies them.

Fitting the knob stile Once I am satisfied with the consistency of the top gap, I joint the top of the door to remove the sawmarks. If I'm installing a single door, I check the side gaps at this point by pushing the door's hinge stile snugly against the case side. This should leave a $\frac{1}{8}$-in. gap between the knob rail and the case side. If necessary, I'll plane the knob rail and then install hinges as described later. If I'm installing a pair of doors, I follow the same procedure with the second door as the first. When fitting the second door, I make sure that the width of the bottom rails at the points where they meet the knob stiles is within $\frac{1}{32}$ in. Although both bottom rails may be tapered, the eye won't notice that as much as the misalignment of the bottom rails at the center of the pair of doors. Also, I carefully match the top gaps of both doors in the opening.

I set both fitted doors in the opening with their hinge rails tight to the case sides and check the center gap between the two doors. If there isn't a consistent $\frac{3}{16}$-in. gap

A KNIFE IS MORE PRECISE THAN A PENCIL. Scribing around the hinge accurately marks its position. Darken the scribe line with a pencil to make the line easier to see when routing away the waste.

from top to bottom, I adjust it with a plane. I don't attempt to establish my final $\frac{1}{8}$-in. gap between the doors until after the hinges are installed. I finish fitting the doors by sanding the edges of the top, bottom, and hinge stile with a sanding block.

Installing Hinges

I cut hinge mortises by wasting away the bulk of the material with a Ryobi laminate-trimming router and a $\frac{1}{4}$-in.-dia. straight bit and then paring to my layout lines with a sharp chisel. The only way I've found to get a consistent and accurate hinge gap, however, is to test my router setup on some scrap. I actually install a hinge, complete with at least one screw for each leaf, and then measure the gap between the scrap pieces. When the gap is $\frac{1}{16}$ in., I know I have the router bit set at the proper depth. Setting the depth is a trial-and-error process, but I can get pretty close the first

Adjusting Problem Doors

No matter how careful I am, I always seem to end up with a door that just doesn't want to cooperate. A corner sticks out here or recedes into the case or a corner droops there. All of the problems, however, usually fall into one of four areas. These areas and the methods for correcting the problems are detailed in the drawings and the text below.

Uneven gap at top or bottom: Sometimes my doors will fit perfectly without hinges, but once installed, the gap becomes uneven along the top or bottom edge, as shown in figure 1. Hinges, even when taken from the same box, may be slightly different in thickness, which affects the side gap and throws an angle into the top and bottom gap. First I'll check the single screw that I've placed in each leaf to hang the door temporarily. If these screws are tight, I'll add the other two screws to each leaf to see if that will pull the door into line. If the door is still out of line, a small shim of sandpaper under one or both screw plates should bring the door back into alignment. The last resort is to rework the hinge mortise.

Hinge stile not in plane: You can install the hinges perfectly and still have one corner of the hinge stile either proud of or sunken below the plane of the door opening. If the door is out by as much as $\frac{1}{16}$ in., this alignment problem can be overcome by offsetting the two remaining screws in the hinge plate, as shown in figure 2. To begin, loosen the first screw that you installed in the offending hinge. Then, to pull a door in, offset the screws in the door side of the hinge plate toward the back of the hole. To push a door out, place the screws hard against the edge of the hole nearest the barrel. After installing the new screws, I usually remove the initial screw until I'm permanently hanging the door so that I don't cancel any leverage my offset screws have gained. Before

reinstalling the removed screw, I plug the hole with toothpicks dipped in glue. Then I redrill the pilot hole, so I don't affect the fit of the door.

Top of knob stile not in plane: If there is twist or wind in the door, the rest of the door may fit perfectly, yet the top of the knob stile might either be recessed or protrude. Because I almost always install magnet catches at the top of my doors, I can locate the magnets to pull or push a door into line (see figure 3). I've generally found nonmagnetic catches have too much play to be effective in aligning doors. In turn, pulling in the top of the stile almost always pulls in the bottom of the stile as well. I can usually correct this problem by gluing a leather button on the door bottom to push this corner back into plane.

Bottom of knob stile not in plane: If the knob stile is recessed at the bottom, a leather button glued to the door will easily correct this problem as mentioned previously. But a protruding knob stile is the most time-consuming problem to correct when fitting doors. My solution is to sand the protruding door flush. The difference in thickness of the tapered stile is only noticeable when the door is open, and even then, most people will not be aware of it.

I mark the amount of protrusion on the edge of the stile with a pencil, using the adjoining door's stile or the door frame as a guide, as shown in figure 4. Then I remove the door from the case and sand the taper with a belt sander. After determining that the doors are in the same plane, I final-sand the tapered door and install the knobs. If the door has an obvious twist to it, the high corners can be belt-sanded down before installation.

Fig. 1: Uneven gap at top or bottom

If the door droops after hinges are installed, a sandpaper shim placed under one or both hinge leaves will open the side gap and level the top and bottom gaps.

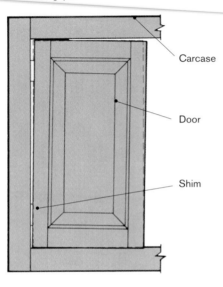

Carcase

Door

Shim

Fig. 3: Top of knob stile not in plane

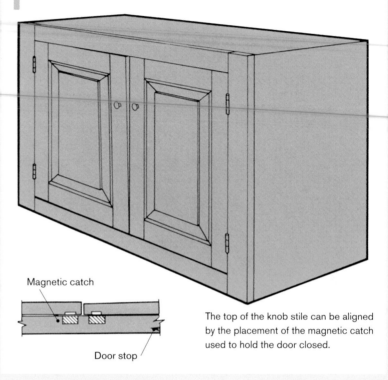

Magnetic catch

Door stop

The top of the knob stile can be aligned by the placement of the magnetic catch used to hold the door closed.

Fig. 2: Hinge stile not in plane

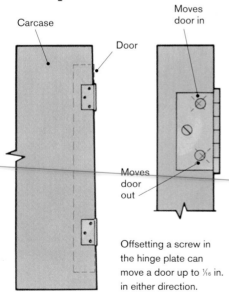

Carcase

Door

Moves door in

Moves door out

Offsetting a screw in the hinge plate can move a door up to 1/16 in. in either direction.

Fig. 4: Bottom of knob stile not in plane

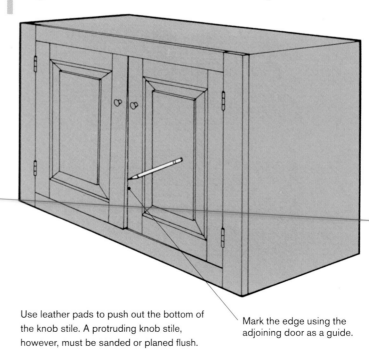

Use leather pads to push out the bottom of the knob stile. A protruding knob stile, however, must be sanded or planed flush.

Mark the edge using the adjoining door as a guide.

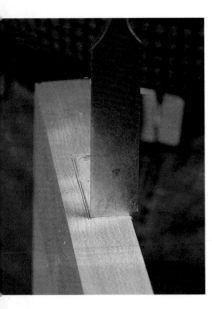

PARE MORTISES GRADUALLY
to the scribed line, alternately
cutting down and from the side.
Be patient, and work slowly for
best results.

time by measuring the thickness of the hinge at the knuckle (the hinges I normally use are ³⁄₁₆ in. thick). From the hinge thickness, I subtract my desired gap and divide by two to get the mortise depth for each hinge leaf.

To install hinges on a door, I start by marking the hinge location. I position hinges so that the top of the top hinge and the bottom of the bottom hinge align with the inside edge of the top and bottom rails, respectively. This establishes the location for the outside shoulder of the hinge. To lay out the hinge mortise, I hold an opened hinge tightly against the hinge rail and scribe around it with a knife, as shown in the photo on p. 105. I use the setup router to remove the majority of waste within the layout lines; then I use a chisel to clean up the shoulders to the knife marks, as shown in the photo at left. It's a good idea to pencil in the scribe lines before routing to make the knife marks more visible. I install both hinges on the door, using just one screw on each leaf. Note that where hinge leaves wrap around the hinge pin, one leaf is notched at the top and bottom and the other leaf is solid. For uniformity, I make it a rule to place the notched leaf on the door and the solid leaf on the case.

To mark the hinge locations on the case, I set the door with hinges installed back in the case opening. I put pennies under the door to re-establish the bottom gap. Holding the door tightly against the case side, I make tick marks on both ends of both hinge barrels with a knife. I remove the door, lay a loose hinge against the tick marks, and scribe around the hinge plate with a knife. I rout and chisel the hinge mortise as before and hang the doors in the case with one screw in each leaf.

Final Adjustments

With the doors screwed in place, I check my gaps along the hinge stiles and at the tops and bottoms around both doors. If everything looks right, I plane the knob stiles of both doors until the center gap between the doors is from ³⁄₃₂ in. to ⅛ in. After I am satisfied that my gaps are consistent and even all around the door opening, I remove the doors. To provide swing clearance for the doors, I joint a slight taper toward the back of the door on the knob stiles of both doors. I drill a hole for the knob, centered on the knob stile and 5 in. down from the top of a base cabinet's door. (On wall or top cabinets, I mount the knob 5 in. from the bottom, and on center cabinets or cabinets on stands, I'll position the knob 2 in. above center.) Then I finish-sand the door and break all the edges with sandpaper.

I reinstall the doors on the case and feel all around the door opening to see that the door is sitting in the opening evenly and that both doors lie flat in plane with each other. If they are satisfactory, I install the remaining screws, knobs, and door catches. After the door is installed and I am happy with everything, I break the edges of the door opening lightly with sandpaper.

This is the procedure I use to fit flush doors at its simplest. It is rare that everything goes this smoothly, though. When things don't turn out, I resort to one or all of the problem-solving techniques discussed in the sidebar on pp. 106-107.

STEVEN BUNN is a woodworker in Bowdoinham, Maine.

Glazing Cabinet Doors

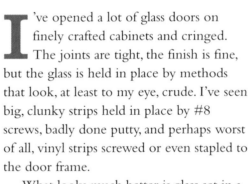

BY TONY KONOVALOFF

I've opened a lot of glass doors on finely crafted cabinets and cringed. The joints are tight, the finish is fine, but the glass is held in place by methods that look, at least to my eye, crude. I've seen big, clunky strips held in place by #8 screws, badly done putty, and perhaps worst of all, vinyl strips screwed or even stapled to the door frame.

What looks much better is glass set in a relatively deep rabbet in the frame and held in place with beveled strips of wood on the back side of the door. The strips function like quarter-round molding, but the profile is more refined. The strips, which are easy to make, are fastened to the shoulder of the rabbet with brass escutcheon pins. Should the glass need to be replaced, the strips easily pop off and can be reused.

Holding glass in a door this way is nothing new. It's an old technique that works because it's simple and practical, and it looks good whether the door is open or closed.

Designing for Glass

With glass-front cabinets, the focus is not on the furniture but on what's inside it. Before you begin making the cabinet, think about how a glass front will affect the design and construction. For instance,

GLASS ADDS A WHOLE NEW DIMENSION TO A CABINET. The inside is as important as the outside. The thin beveled strips holding the glass to the back of these doors looks good from either side.

Building the Frame

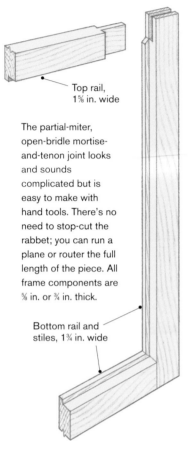

Top rail,
1⅝ in. wide

The partial-miter, open-bridle mortise-and-tenon joint looks and sounds complicated but is easy to make with hand tools. There's no need to stop-cut the rabbet; you can run a plane or router the full length of the piece. All frame components are ⅝ in. or ¾ in. thick.

Bottom rail and stiles, 1¾ in. wide

THE STRIP ON THE LEFT IS READY TO INSTALL. **The bevel and chamfers, though small, are obvious when compared with the rectangular strip on the right.**

everything is now visible, so the layout and fit of the joints on the inside of the cabinet are as important as those on the outside.

Glass thickness and temper Standard window glass is only ³⁄₃₂ in. thick, and I use it almost exclusively. It's called single-thickness float glass, and I buy it cut to order at a local glass shop. When safety is a factor (when the glass will be near the floor in a household with children, for example), I use tempered glass. The thinnest readily available size of tempered glass is ⅛ in., and it has to be special-ordered.

I wouldn't use beveled strips where the glass is thicker than ⅛ in. because the rails and the stiles must be beefed up to accommodate the glass and the larger strips. Unless the cabinet is really large, the whole thing probably will look clumsy.

Glass weighs about three times as much as wood. But the weight of a simple door glazed with ³⁄₃₂-in. or ⅛-in. glass is roughly the same as that of a similar wooden panel door because the glass is so much thinner. There's no need to consider special hinges or hardware.

Attaching the Beveled Strips

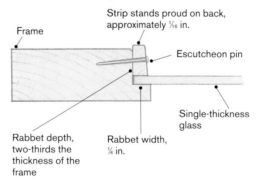

Frame

Strip stands proud on back, approximately ¹⁄₁₆ in.

Escutcheon pin

Single-thickness glass

Rabbet depth, two-thirds the thickness of the frame

Rabbet width, ¼ in.

Glass color and wood choice Standard float glass, sometimes called soda-lime float glass, has a slight green tinge. The effect is more noticeable as the thickness of the glass increases, and it can alter the color of the wood behind it. Sometimes the effect can be pleasing, and sometimes it's not. Test it by looking at wood samples through the glass you intend to use.

Dimensions and construction of frames When sizing the cabinet-door frames, keep in mind that the clear front affects the apparent widths of the frame pieces. The same size frame you'd use for a wooden panel front looks too heavy with glass.

When I make a medium-sized cabinet door (something like 15 in. wide by 24 in. tall), the frame pieces are ⅝ in. or ¾ in. thick, depending on the thickness of the glass. I make the bottom rail and the stiles 1¾ in. wide, with the top rail ⅛ in. narrower. The rabbet depth is two-thirds the thickness of the frame.

I join my frames with a partial-miter, open-bridle mortise and tenon. It's a long-winded name for something quite simple (see the drawing at far left). It's an old molding joint that saves the trouble of stop-cutting the rabbets. The joint is quick and easy to do with hand tools (which are all I use), because you can cut the joint first and then run the rabbet the full length of the piece. It's also an attractive joint.

Another way to join the frames is to glue up a doweled (or biscuited) frame and run a rabbet around the inside with a router, squaring up the corners with a chisel. It really doesn't matter how the frames are made as long as you plan for the rabbet.

Installing the Glass

When the doors are made but not finished, I take them to the local glass shop to have the glass fitted. A good slip fit is desirable for the glass—if it's loose in the frame, it may rattle when a truck drives by. There's no need to allow for movement in either the wood or the glass in a medium-sized door.

If the glass is too snug in the frame, adjust the fit with a rabbet plane and a bull-nose rabbet plane. If the glass is a little small, you can shim out the rabbets with thin slivers of wood. Nothing will show once the beveled strips are in place. Once the glass fits correctly, I turn my attention back to the door. I fit it to the carcase and install the hinges and catches. Then I finish the door (inside and out) and set it aside.

Fitting the beveled strips The beveled strips are sized so that when they're installed, they will stand slightly proud of the frame and be a little narrower than the rabbet (see the bottom drawing on the facing

Shaping Beveled Strips to Keep Glass in Place

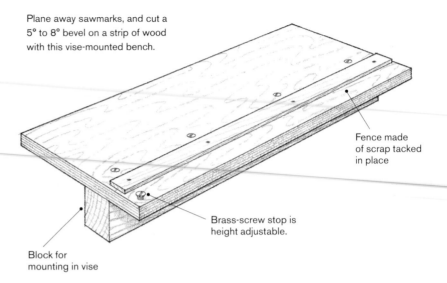

Plane away sawmarks, and cut a 5° to 8° bevel on a strip of wood with this vise-mounted bench.

Fence made of scrap tacked in place

Brass-screw stop is height adjustable.

Block for mounting in vise

USING THE MINI-BENCH. A screw keeps the strip in place while the author planes a 5° to 8° bevel.

CHAMFERING THE BEVELED STRIPS relieves any sharp edges.

page). The strips are not rectangular in section—they bevel about 5° to 8° (see the photo on p. 110). This makes them less visible from the outside.

I rip the strips from long scraps of the same wood as the frame. I plane all four sides (including the bevel) on a small vise-mounted bench I built for handling small pieces (see the drawing and photo at left on p. 111). It has an adjustable stop made from a brass screw and a light fence tacked on to hold the strips for planing. Then I lightly chamfer all the edges with a small spoke-shave (see the photo at right on p. 111).

When the finish on the door is dry, I lay it on the bench, set the glass in the rabbet, and fit the strips: first the top and bottom strips and then the sides. I cut them a little long with a backsaw and then pare them to fit with a chisel (see the photo below). Because of the bevel, the side pieces aren't cut at a right angle. The best way to fit them is by paring away a little at a time. Once the strips are fitted, I lightly file the corners to match the chamfer on the other pieces.

USE A CHISEL TO PARE THE ENDS OF THE STRIPS TO FIT after cutting them a little long with a backsaw.

Fastening the Strips

I prefer escutcheon pins over brads for holding the strips in place. I like the look of the brass head, and the pins make a more secure fastening. I use #18 escutcheon pins, ⅝ in. long.

Getting Clear on Glass
BY AIMÉ FRASER

People who work with glass have their own language, and the terms don't necessarily coincide with common usage. As glass formulations and manufacturing change, so do the words. Here's a partial list to make it easier to talk with your glazier.

PLATE GLASS

These days, plate glass is a generic term for sheet glass, but it has a more specific meaning to glaziers. To them, it refers to sheet goods produced by running molten glass through rollers and then lapping and polishing it on both sides. This is the way most glass was made prior to the 1960s, but it is a labor-intensive process. Plate glass is used now only for high-quality optical glass.

FLOAT GLASS

About 30 years ago, a new manufacturing process was perfected that fully automated the production of flat and virtually distortion-free glass. A plant easily can manufacture a nearly perfect sheet of glass 4 ft. wide and a quarter of a mile long. Today, the bulk of commonly available glass is produced this way.

With the strips fitted in place, I mark the locations of the escutcheon pins every 4 in. to 5 in. I remove the strips and drill the shank holes for a push fit. I use a #53 (0.059 in.) or #54 drill (0.055 in.), depending on the wood. Check the fit in a piece of scrap to be sure. I drill the holes at right angles to the bevel and clean up both sides of the hole by turning a small countersink a few times by hand (see the top photo on p. 114).

DOUBLE-THICKNESS SODA-LIME float glass (top) has a slightly green tinge. Water-white glass of the same thickness (bottom) has almost no color.

The whole process takes place in a giant oven. Molten glass is poured onto a pool of molten tin, where it levels itself out. It cools slightly and is slid off the tin and into an annealing oven. From there, it is reheated to just below the melting point and then cooled slowly to relieve internal stresses. When annealed glass breaks, it breaks into large, irregular sharp shards.

TEMPERED GLASS

It is possible to temper glass and alter its breaking characteristics so that it breaks into small, relatively harmless pieces. In the bargain, the glass is strengthened. The downside is that once tempered, the glass cannot be drilled, cut or even nicked without shattering into tiny pieces.

Tempered glass starts as annealed glass that is cut and machined to its finished dimensions. It's put into the oven and heated once more, almost to the melting point. Then it's quickly cooled on one side by jets of chilled air, which causes rapid hardening of the glass on that side; the other side is still red hot. This builds a great deal of stress into the glass, so when it breaks, it shatters into thousands of pieces. Each one is the size of the area cooled by one jet.

On thick glass, this process causes no distortion. But it can cause thinner or smaller pieces of glass to curl like a potato chip. For this reason, glass less than ⅛ in. thick is usually tempered chemically. It's not as strong as heat-tempered glass, and it breaks into larger pieces.

LEADED GLASS

The color of the glass is determined by the mineral content of the sand it's made from. Each sand quarry produces glass of a slightly different color, which can be altered by the addition or extraction of various mineral oxides. The green color of common glass is from iron oxide. When this mineral is removed, the glass has almost no color. The addition of lead will further enhance clarity, but leaded glass cannot be produced by the float method. It must be lapped and polished; however, the process does produce optical-quality glass for lenses and prisms.

SINGLE-THICKNESS GLASS

Glass is manufactured in a variety of thicknesses from 0.0394 in. (1mm) up to several inches. Most glass is ³⁄₃₂ in. thick. The industry has designated this single thickness, whether or not it has been tempered.

DOUBLE-THICKNESS GLASS

For some reason, ⅛-in.-thick glass is commonly known as double thickness, even though this glass is only ¹⁄₃₂ in. thicker than single-thickness glass.

AIMÉ FRASER, fomerly an assistant editor at *Fine Woodworking* magazine, is the author of *Getting Started in Woodworking*.

CLEAN UP BOTH SIDES of the escutcheon-pin shank holes by hand-turning a small countersink.

I put the escutcheon pins partway in the shank holes in the strips and put the strips back in place on the glass. Holding the strip firmly in place, I lightly tap each pin to mark the frame for the pilot holes. After removing the strips and the glass, I use the marks in the frame as centers for drilling the pilot holes. I use a #55 drill (0.052) for a hammer fit, and I drill at about 5° off the perpendicular—the amount of the bevel.

Everything is ready for final assembly, but first I finish both the strips and the inside of the cabinet with paste wax.

Final Assembly

Before installing the glass, I clean it one last time. I put it back in the frame, put the strips in place, and protect the glass with a piece of cardboard cut from a cereal box. I set the escutcheon pins with a 3-oz.

Warrington hammer; it's light and narrow, perfect for such delicate work (see the photo below). Don't try to drive the pins in one blow—take it slowly. Be careful not to hit the strips, or they'll be marred by the hammer.

If an escutcheon pin goes into the frame too easily because the diameter of the pilot hole is a little too big or the hole too deep, you can tighten it up by bending the pin. Just hit it with the other end of a Warrington hammer to put in a slight curve. When you put the pin back in the pilot hole, it'll snug up nicely.

Because I've already fit and finished the door, all that's left is to mount it in the cabinet. After this is done, I install a small riser in each door opening to support the doors when closed. Risers are pieces of wood, ¼ in. by ¼ in. by ⅜ in. long, mortised into the cabinet bottom on the catch side. The block goes in end grain up and is filed down until its height equals the gap between the carcase and the door (about the thickness of a business card). The door rests lightly on the riser and opens and closes freely.

TONY KONOVALOFF is a professional furniture maker in Oak Harbor, Washington.

PROTECT THE GLASS WITH CARDBOARD, and carefully use a light hammer when setting the escutcheon pins.

Arched Top Cabinet Doors

BY BILL EWING

In woodworking, as in architecture, arches can be both decorative and functional. Positioned below the main structure, an arch adds strength without the visual weight of heftier underpinnings. Placed higher up, such as in the upper rail of a bookcase, an arch lends a bit of elegance. Adding an arch to the upper rail of a cabinet door is also an easy way to refine the sometimes boxy look of frame-and-panel construction.

I wanted to find a quick way to cut arched doors so that I could offer this design option to my clients. After a little planning and experimentation, and in one quick afternoon, I was able to make an adjustable jig that allows me to cut arched raised-panel doors of almost any size. The few hours spent building the jig proved worth the time; over the last four years, I've used it to make countless doors for the kitchen cabinets that are the mainstay of my business.

The only way to get uniformly fair arches is to work from two accurate templates—one for the rail and one for the panel. Each door width also requires a different set of templates. Using the two-piece jig shown on pp. 116–117, I can quickly and efficiently cut a set of panel and rail

IT'S EASY TO MAKE arched raised-panel doors of any size with an adjustable jig and a router.

templates to fit a wide range of cabinet-door sizes. By using these templates in conjunction with rail- and stile-cutting bits, you can cut the door parts for a whole set of kitchen cabinets in a day.

The key to this jig is that it can be adjusted in two different ways. The radius arm of the jig allows you to make arcs of different radii. The sliding pivot point in the base allows you to move the center point of the arc's radius to accommodate varying widths of door rails. Another great thing about this jig is that it can be adjusted while the router is in place. To cut out the panel and rail templates, I always use a plunge router with a ¼-in. straight bit.

A 1-in. Arch Looks Best on Cabinet Doors

Before making panel and rail templates, you have to establish a few design parameters: the depth of the arch and the width of the rail. After some experimentation, I've found that a 1-in. arch looks best on most cabinet doors. An arch of less than 1 in. leaves the rail too meaty and the arch too subtle. Making an arch with a depth of more than 1 in. cuts down on rail width so much that it appears weakened.

For both aesthetics and uniformity, I always use 2⅜ in. for my rail and stile widths. I maintain this 2⅜-in. dimension at the midpoint of the arc and increase this measurement by 1 in. at each end of the rail. These measurements remain constant regardless of the rail length.

Templates Are Easy to Make

Once the jig is up and running, you're ready to make templates. While it's possible to determine the measurements by trial and error each time you set out to make a template, I refer to a graph (see the sidebar on p. 118) that tells the radius and pivot-point measurements needed to cut templates for various rail lengths. If I need to cut an arch with a depth of other than 1 in., I use the simple formula to gauge the radius.

Adjustable Jig

The radius arm

The radius arm consists of a piece of hardwood, a wooden circle, and a piece of Masonite. Slots in the arm, which accept the adjustable pivot point, are cut on a router table. A tenon at the end of the arm fits into a mortise in the wooden circle. Stick-on measuring tape measures the distance between the pivot point and the router bit. The Masonite backing adds strength and provides a base for the router.

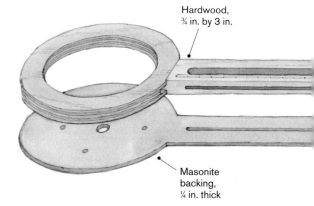

Hardwood,
¾ in. by 3 in.

Masonite
backing,
¼ in. thick

The base

The main body of the jig base is made of ¾-in. plywood with routed slots that house the sliding pivot point. The 4-in.-wide recessed template well is as deep as the template material is thick—¼ in. on this jig. Rail templates butt the top of the well; panel templates butt the bottom. The bottom of the base is covered with Masonite.

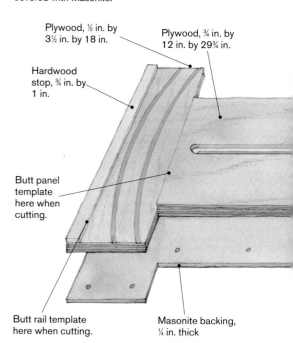

Plywood, ½ in. by 3½ in. by 18 in.

Plywood, ¾ in. by 12 in. by 29¾ in.

Hardwood stop, ¾ in. by 1 in.

Butt panel template here when cutting.

Butt rail template here when cutting.

Masonite backing, ¼ in. thick

Sliding pivot points

The sliding pivot points in the base and the radius arm must fit snugly into their corresponding slots. The author puts a ⁵⁄₃₂-in. brass rod in the radius arm's pivot point and a mating brass tube in the base's pivot point. The rod and tube provide a smooth, precise connection between the radius arm and the jig base. Rod and tubing can be found at most hobby shops.

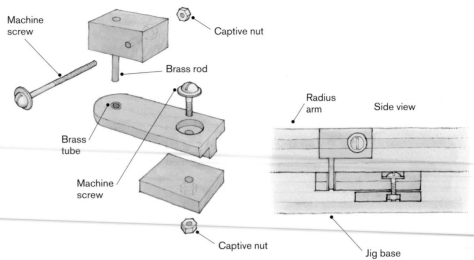

Machine screw

Captive nut

Brass rod

Brass tube

Machine screw

Captive nut

Radius arm

Side view

Jig base

Measuring tape

Pivot point in radius arm

Pivot point in jig base

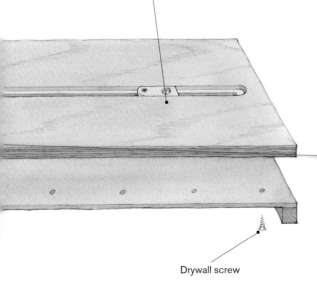

Drywall screw

Jigs Cut Templates That Help Build Doors

To build arched raised-panel doors, you must have two templates—one for the panel and one for the rail. The author's jig adjusts so that you can cut a matching set of templates. The templates are used to cut fair and complementary curves on a door's panel and rail.

Routing the Templates

MAKING THE RAIL TEMPLATE. With brads securing the template blank in place, a router outfitted with a ¼-in. straight bit cuts a smooth arch in the rail template.

SLIGHT ADJUSTMENT. To cut the panel template, increase the radius on the jig's arm ½ in. to allow for the bit diameter and the panel tongue.

A MATCHING PAIR. Once the radius has been adjusted, tack a Masonite blank onto the jig's well. Cut the panel template with the router in a single pass.

FINDING THE PERFECT CURVE

When you have to handle different-sized arches in a single piece of furniture or in a set of cabinets, it's imperative that the height of the arches be uniform. Even small irregularities in the arches can be seen at a glance.

It's possible to use trial and error to determine the measurements each time you make a template of different rail lengths, but I plotted points on a graph that allow me to see quickly what the radius of the arc needs to be. These measurements will give you a height of 1 in., a suitable arch for most cabinets.

Radii for common rail lengths

Rail length	Radius
6 in.	5 in.
7 in.	6.625 in.
8 in.	8.5 in.
9 in.	10.625 in.
10 in.	13 in.
11 in.	15.625 in.
12 in.	18.5 in.
13 in.	21.625 in.
14 in.	25 in.
15 in.	28.625 in.
16 in.	32.5 in.

(Graph: Radius (inches) on vertical axis from 5 to 28, Rail length (inches) on horizontal axis from 6 to 15, showing plotted points along a rising curve.)

Formula for success

I once had to build doors that required an arch with a radius longer than my jig could handle. I found the radius through trial and error—not my favorite method. Since then, I've avoided the trial of all of these errors using a simple algebra formula my son-in-law (an engineer) derived:

$$R^2 = (R-X)^2 + (L/2)^2,$$

Where R = arc radius,

L = cord (the distance between the ends of the arc),

X = height at the midpoint of the arc.

Don't panic—the formula reduces to a more manageable size when you substitute the height of the door arch (in this case, 1 in.) for X. It becomes:

$$R = \tfrac{1}{2} + L^2/8.$$

For example, if your rail length is 8 in.:

$$R = \tfrac{1}{2} + 8^2/8,$$

$$R = \tfrac{1}{2} + 64/8,$$

$$R = 8\tfrac{1}{2} \text{ in.}$$

For arch heights other than 1 in., such as in the top face frame of a display cabinet, just substitute the desired height for X. I've crunched the numbers for 2-in., 3-in., and 4-in. heights.

2 in.: $R = 1 + L^2/16$;

3 in.: $R = \tfrac{3}{8} = L^2/24$;

4 in.: $R = 2 + L^2/32$.

To make a rail template, first install a ¼-in. Masonite template blank—3½ in. wide and 2 in. longer than the rail length—against the hardwood stop in the recessed well on the jig's base. Set the brass rod in the radius-arm pivot point into the brass tube in the base's pivot point. The pivot point on the radius arm slides and is secured with a machine screw on the side of the arm. Loosen the screw, and move the pivot point to the correct rail length, then retighten it. Then loosen the adjustment screw on the pivot point in the base and retighten it slightly shy of its final position. Measure the distance between the ends of the arc and keep adjusting the pivot point on the jig's base until this end-to-end measurement equals the desired rail length. Now you're ready to rout the arch.

Once the rail template has been cut, move on to the panel template. The arc for the panel template will have to be slightly larger than that of the rail template. As you move from making the rail template to making the panel template, you must in-crease the length of the radius to accom-modate the bit diameter because the router is cutting on the opposite side of the bit. You also have to lengthen the radius arm to create a tongue on the panel.

Lengthen the radius arm by ½ in. to compensate for the ¼-in. bit diameter and ¼-in. panel tongue. Start with a template blank that is 3 in. wide and the same length as the rail template. Butt it against the rear stop and attach it with brads. Once the pivot point has been adjusted, simply rout the arc. After cutting the templates, you can start building doors.

Build Doors Oversized and Trim Them to Fit

Somewhere, perhaps in a parallel universe, frame-and-panel doors always glue up square, and the stile ends are always even with the rails. But in my shop, reality reigns.

To correct minor imperfections in assembly, I build my doors ¼ in. long—adding ⅛ in. to the width of both the top and bottom rails—and trim them to size with a crosscut sled on my table saw.

Using the table saw, cut stock for the upper and lower rail 3½ in. and 2½ in. wide, respectively, and leave them ½ in. longer than the finished length. Because each stile is 2⅜ in. wide and you lose ⅜ in. of each edge when you cut the inner edge profile, the rail length is 4 in. less than the overall door width. Cut the stiles 2⅜ in. wide and ¼ in. longer than the finished door height.

Rail-Cutting Sequence Is Key

It is important to follow a particular se-quence when shaping the rails and stiles because you could end up trying to shape the upper rail ends without a straight edge to rest against the router table's miter gauge, or you could encounter serious chipout problems when the stile-cutting bit exits the arch in the upper rail.

Place the rail template on the back of the upper rail and align the end of the arch with the left (when viewed from the front) end of the rail and draw the arc. With a rail-cutting bit in your router table, shape the left end of the upper rail and the right end of the bottom rail.

Remove the waste material on a band-saw, tack the template into position, and shape the rail's arch on the router table using the stile-cutting bit with a pilot bearing on top. This is a small piece to cut on a router table, so use a hold-down jig. While the bit is still in place, go ahead and shape the in-side edges of the stiles and lower rail, as well as a scrap piece of the same stock to be used in dry-fitting the panel. Finally, cut the upper rail and lower rail to length on a table saw or miter box. The only thing left is to replace the stile-cutting bit with the rail-cutting bit and shape the remaining rail ends.

Shaping the Rail

ROUGHING OUT THE RAIL. Shape one end of the rail on the router table, then cut away the excess material on the bandsaw.

CUT THE PROFILE AND CURVE IN ONE PASS. With the template tacked into place, use a rail-cutting bit to shape the profile and fair the edge.

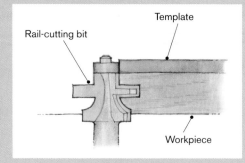

Template

Rail-cutting bit

Workpiece

A Dry Run Avoids Headaches

Dry-fitting the frame allows you to take exact measurements for the panel. Be sure to allow for a ¼-in. tongue on all four edges. Rip the panel to exact width so that the arch of the panel will match up with that of the rail. Leave the length of the panel about 1 in. long so that the arch doesn't have to be cut to the very edge of the panel.

Using a framing square, draw a line across the back of the panel, approximately 1½ in. from the top. Use the square to align the arch of the panel template with the line you've just drawn, making sure that it meets each edge of the panel, and draw the arc. Rough-cut the panel's arch on the bandsaw and tack the template back into place. To ensure a nice, smooth edge, clean up the cut with a bearing-driven straight bit on your router table, and trim the panel to finished length.

Now you can shape the panel using a panel-raising bit with a top-mounted pilot bearing. Use the fence in the normal fashion for the straight edges. As you shape the curved edge, register the panel against both the fence and the pilot bearing. This is safe, provided the panel is large enough to grip firmly and you don't try to hog off too much material in a single pass. Use a scrap piece of stile stock to check that you raise the panel to the correct depth.

All that remains is to cut the back rabbet in the panel so that it fits the groove in the rails and stiles. Once everything falls into place, some glue and a couple of clamps bring everything together. Measure the door's exact length off the cabinet and trim the door to length. When you hang the door, the elegant arch serves as a subtle reminder that it was designed with care.

BILL EWING is a cabinetmaker in Girard, Ohio.

Shaping the Panel

CUT THE PANEL TO ROUGH SHAPE. Trace the arc from the template onto the panel and trim the waste material away on the bandsaw.

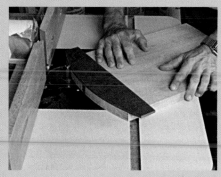

TRIM THE PANEL FLUSH. **Tack the template in place and trim the panel flush on the router table using a straight bit with a pilot bearing.**

RAISE THE PANEL. **When turning a flat panel into a raised one, you can make a safer cut by using both the fence and the pilot bearing.**

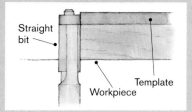

Straight bit
Template
Workpiece

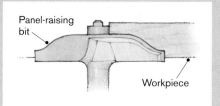

Panel-raising bit
Workpiece

Arched Grain for Arched Doors

When you build custom arched doors, you have the opportunity to use grain that accentuates the design. My general guidelines are simple—straight grain for the frames and more striking grain patterns for the panels.

For the upper rail of an arched door, look for grain with a slight curve that follows the curve of the arch. Don't expect a perfect match, but any slight curve in the grain will help.

Laying out the grain pattern for a door panel is more complex. In general, look for a grain pattern that arches upward so that it draws your eye to the arch in the door. This grain pattern is common in most flatsawn lumber.

GOOD GRAIN, BAD GRAIN. Whenever possible, the grain patterns should echo the arch (above) rather than fight it (below).

Smooth Tambours

BY MIKE WEISS

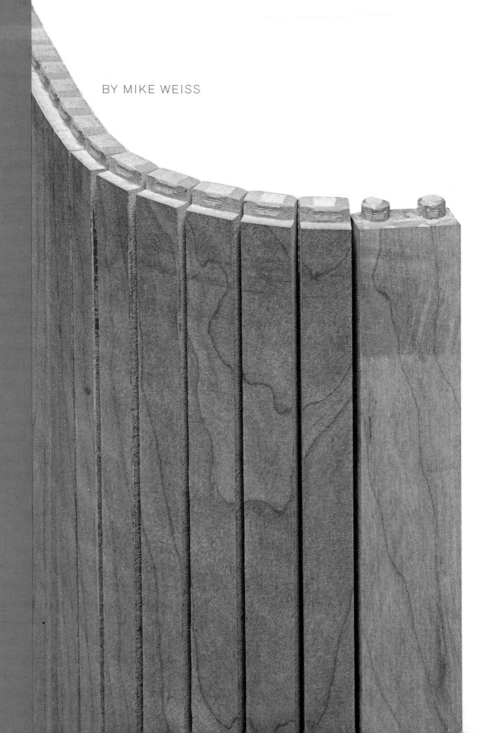

Tambours are universally recognized for their rounded, canvas-backed slats and may be found on everything from rolltop desks to appliance garages. But there's a lesser-known type of tambour that masquerades as a smooth, solid-wood door. The first time I came across a door constructed this way, I pulled on it, assuming it was hinged, to the amusement of the desk's owner.

Suitably impressed with the illusion, I set out to make a set of these tambours for a contemporary entertainment center. My tambours are made of veneered medium-density fiberboard (MDF) cut into slats and held together by canvas, like traditional tambours. The biggest challenge of this project was figuring out how to rip apart the slats with minimal kerf loss and without interrupting the grain on the front of the tambours.

Tambours Demand Lots of Planning

When building tambours, allowances must be made for the considerable loss of material that results from ripping stock into lots of narrow slats. Then the slats must be dimensioned so that they operate smoothly when going around the interior corner of the case.

Designing a Cabinet for Tambours

A cabinet made for tambours requires a track on the inside top and bottom panels. The track must break through the rear on one side of the cabinet so that the tambours may be installed. To ensure that the tambours slide smoothly in their tracks, use a template when routing the grooves so that both the top and bottom tracks are exactly in line.

To hide the back of the tambours when they are opened, I add two partition panels dadoed into the top and bottom of the cabinet and slid in from the rear. I also place two panels at the front of the cabinet on both sides of the tambours.

By hiding the corner of the tambours, the doors simply disappear into the case as they are opened.

THE FINISHED CABINET APPEARS TO HAVE SOLID-WOOD DOORS. The panels on both edges conceal the parting of the slats as the doors are opened.

SEE HOW THEY RUN. With the back of the cabinet removed (far left), the two tambours can be fed in from the right rear side and slid around to their respective positions. Then the two partition panels are fitted so that the tambours are concealed when the doors slide into the case (left).

And the end slat should be double the width of the others so that a handle may be attached.

I used a full-sized drawing to figure out the dimensions. The slats for the entertainment center are ⅝ in. wide with ¹¹⁄₃₂-in.-thick pins, which ride in the tracks. The end slats (handle attachment points) are 1⅜ in. wide. The tracks are ⅜ in. wide to allow for smooth operation without excessive play. Where each track enters the case, it makes a 90° bend through a 2-in. radius.

Veneer the Back and Cut Slats

Use ½-in.-thick MDF as the substrate for the slats. MDF is stiff enough for doors of this size (31½ in. high), and the material's uniform density allows it to hold up well where it makes contact with the track.

To begin, cut an MDF panel oversized and glue a backing veneer to one side. The substrate must be veneered on both sides to prevent it from warping (the face veneer goes on later).

Next, rip the panel into slats. I made up a double-thickness push stick that allowed me to apply uniform pressure on both sides of the sawblade. The added control of such a push stick produces clean cuts. After cutting, number the slats on their ends and sand away any saw marks. When assembled in order, it is critical that the slats fit together tightly; otherwise, excess glue may find its way into the gaps when applying the face veneer.

1. Rip the Panel into Slats

Backing veneer is applied to the over-sized ½-in.-thick MDF door panel.

MDF cut into ⅝-in.-wide slats

CUT THE SLATS. After applying backing veneer to one side, rip the panel into slats. A double-width push stick and a slow, steady feed rate help keep the slat tight against the fence.

Glue the Face Veneer onto the Slats

To hold the slats in position, I built a jig from two layers of ½-in.-thick MDF. The jig is slightly oversized to allow for sawing the slats to the final length. A wedge provides clamping pressure to the slats. And to prevent damage to the veneer bag, I rounded over all the hard edges of the jig. I have used two-part liquid urea resin glue for its slow setting properties, but on this occasion I used yellow glue. Once the slats are all positioned tightly together, spread the glue, lay on the face veneer, and place the assembly into a vacuum press.

After carefully removing the door from the vacuum press (remember, it is a bunch of individual slats joined together only by a continuous sheet of face veneer), trim the face veneer flush with the substrate using a router. Moisten the veneer tape with water, then scrape and sand away the tape and any traces of glue.

Trim the Face Veneer with a Knife

I achieve the nearly seamless appearance of the tambours by cutting apart the slats using a fine knife and another jig. The jig employs an acrylic rod partially embedded in a piece of MDF.

To cut the face veneer, place the slat assembly on the jig, backside up. Then flex apart two adjacent slats over the length of the acrylic rod, and cut the veneer using an X-Acto knife. Gentle pressure with repeated strokes seems to produce the cleanest cuts. Replace the blade often, and rotate the acrylic rod slightly for each new cut so there is a fresh, smooth surface supporting the veneer as it is sliced.

Apply the Canvas, Machine the Pins, Then Apply a Finish

Once the slats have been separated and the edges cleaned of any glue, reassemble them in the holding jig face veneer down. Then add the solid-wood handle-attachment slat to one end of the tambour. Because you are unlikely to find a piece of solid stock to match the face veneer, you may want to make the handle slat contrast with the rest of the door.

For the backer, I use 12-oz. artist's canvas, cut slightly wider than needed, and fasten it with yellow glue. To prevent the canvas from sticking to the vacuum bag, place melamine-coated particleboard or plywood over it.

With the glue-up completed, cut the tambour to its final size on the table saw. Then machine the rabbets on the upper and lower edges to form the pins, which

2. Glue on the Face Veneer

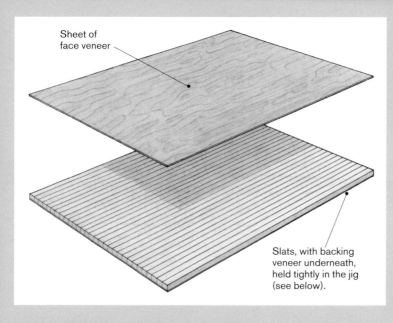

Sheet of face veneer

Slats, with backing veneer underneath, held tightly in the jig (see below).

ROLL AN EVEN COAT OF YELLOW GLUE ONTO THE SLATS IN THE JIG. Carefully align the face veneer, top with a caul of melamine-coated particleboard, and place the assembly in the vacuum press.

Simple jig keeps slats aligned

THE JIG IS MADE from two layers of ½-in.-thick MDF. The tambour slats are held tight by a sliding wedge that is tapped home.

AFTER THE GLUE HAS SET, TRIM THE FACE VENEER. Use a router and a flush-trimming bit to remove the face-veneer overhang. To remove the veneer tape, first moisten it with water, then scrape it off.

3. Slice Apart the Slats and Glue on the Backing

APPLY THE CANVAS BACKING. Cut the canvas a little oversized to allow for shrinking after the glue dries. The slats are held tight in the same jig used for applying the face veneer.

CUT THE PINS. Because the slats are held together only by the canvas, an antikickback device applies downward pressure while the pins are cut. Featherboards would work, too.

REDUCE THE DRAG. Chamfer the front edges of the top and bottom pins. In addition, ease the side edges of the bottom pins.

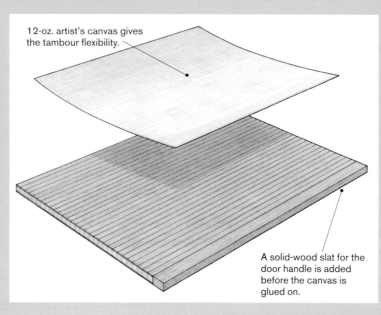

12-oz. artist's canvas gives the tambour flexibility.

A solid-wood slat for the door handle is added before the canvas is glued on.

The key to continuous grain

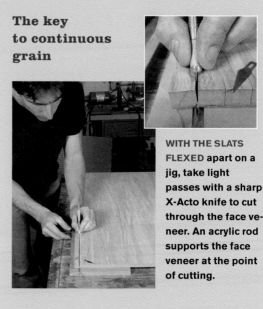

WITH THE SLATS FLEXED apart on a jig, take light passes with a sharp X-Acto knife to cut through the face veneer. An acrylic rod supports the face veneer at the point of cutting.

guide the door along the tracks. Cut the rabbets on the faces of the tambours so that the panel overhangs the bottom track, hiding it, when the tambours are shut.

To minimize friction, chamfer the front edges of all the pins with a chisel. Additionally, ease the side edges of the bottom pins.

I sprayed a lacquer finish on the tambours and cabinet shown here. If you use a rubbed-on finish, I suggest that you place

the tambours in the jig to keep the slats tight and to lessen the chances of tearing an edge of the face veneer.

After the finish is dry, apply wax to the pins and track to further reduce friction. Last, glue a narrow strip of wood to the back of the hardwood handle slat to cover the edge of the backing canvas.

MIKE WEISS is a woodworker in Delaware County, New York.

Making a Drawer with Half-Blind Dovetails

HALF-BLIND DOVETAILS ALLOW DRAWERS TO BLEND IN with surrounding surfaces and make for continuous grain pattern or figure, top to bottom and side to side across a piece. The joint is no more difficult to cut than through-dovetails.

When I make drawers, I use half-blind dovetails to join the drawer front to the sides. I'm a traditionalist and prefer not to let the joint show through on the face of a piece. To enhance the look of the joinery when the drawer is pulled open, I use two contrasting woods on my drawers, such as walnut for the front and white ash for the sides and back.

Once I've selected the wood, dimensioned it, and cut it to size, I mark each board to indicate which edge is up, what part of the drawer it is (left side, right side, or back), and which face is outside. I look at the grain pattern and growth rings, and I make sure the inside of the tree is on the outside of my work. Then I cut a groove near the bottom of the drawer sides and front with a couple of passes on my table saw, making it a snug fit for the drawer

bottom. I test the fit with a piece of scrap the same thickness as the drawer bottom. I rip the drawer back to the top of the groove, so I can slide the drawer bottom in after assembly.

Next, I set my marking gauge to the thickness of the drawer sides. Then I mark the inside of the drawer front, all around both ends of the drawer back and around the back ends of the two drawer sides, which will be through-dovetailed to the back. I set my marking gauge to about two-thirds the thickness of the drawer front (the tail length), and I mark the two ends of the drawer front.

Then I cut and chisel my dovetails as shown in detail on the next three pages. Once all the pieces are cut, I test-fit them and make any necessary adjustments. Then I disassemble the pieces, finish the inside surfaces with a few strokes of a fine smoothing

MAKING A DRAWER WITH HALF-BLIND DOVETAILS   127

plane, and sand them with 120-grit sand-paper. I apply white glue with a disposable acid brush. I've found that white glue sets a bit slower than yellow glue, so I don't have to rush the assembly. The brush helps me get a good, even coat, even in tight spaces.

I don't use clamps on drawers; the joints are tight enough to create a good bond between the drawer parts. I use a hammer and a block of hardwood to close the joints. To ensure that the drawers are square, I just insert the drawer bottom as soon as the drawer is together. Because the bottom is square, the drawer squares up automatically.

FRANK KLAUSZ makes furniture and repairs antiques at his shop in Pluckemin, New Jersey.

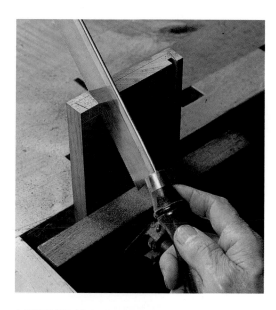

2. NEXT, JUDGE ANGLE AND SPACING BY EYE, without laying out the dovetails, and cut a full tail.

1. CUT THE TWO HALF-PINS at either edge of the drawer-front end, taking care not to cut past either scored line.

3. VISUALLY DIVIDE THE REMAINING SPACE in half for a drawer with two full pins, in thirds for a drawer with three full pins, and so on. Make all cuts at one angle first (see the drawing on the facing page for sequence), and then cut all the opposing angles. Also cut the pins for the drawer back at this time, using the same method. For the strongest dovetail joint, through- or half-blind, pins and tails should be approximately the same size.

5. POSITION YOUR CHISEL 45° AWAY FROM YOUR BODY, about halfway between baseline and the end of the board, bevel up. Whack the chisel with a mallet, gradually moving the chisel back to the end of the board, working down through the waste between the pins.

4. CHISEL BASELINE. Position a paring chisel just ahead of the baseline, bevel out. Tap the chisel with the mallet. The bevel drives the chisel to the scored line, preventing tearout.

6. ALTERNATE CHISELING FROM THE END with perpendicular blows at the baseline that free the waste.

Pin-cutting sequence

By spacing his dovetails by eye, the author saves layout time and ends up with dovetails that are still just as regularly spaced as they need to be. If they're slightly off, so much the better: They look more hand-cut.

Tail depth is approximately two-thirds the thickness of the drawer front.

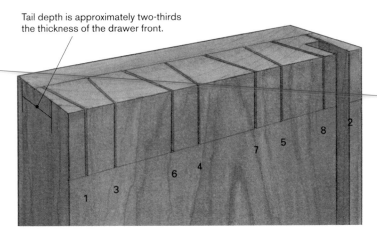

7. CLEAN UP ANY ROUGH PINS once you're down to the tail-depth line (undercut it slightly) by paring carefully into the corners.

8. MARK THE TAILS FROM THE PINS with a sharp pencil. The pencil line is easier to see than a knife line. By splitting the pencil line, you can get as tight a joint as if you'd used a knife. Before doing any marking, though, make sure the inside of the drawer is facing up on the bench and that the groove for the drawer bottom in the side lines up with the groove in the front. After marking the tails on the front of the drawer sides from the drawer front, mark the tails on the rear of the drawer sides from the pins you cut for the drawer back.

9. USE YOUR THUMB TO GUIDE THE BLADE. With the tails marked, put one drawer side upright in the vise with the inside facing you. Take a couple of strokes to establish a kerf at what looks to be the correct angle. Then double-check the angle before finishing the kerf. (Klausz doesn't worry about the blade being horizontal front to back because it's become second nature to him by now.) Saw carefully, splitting the pencil mark just down to the baseline. After repeating the process for both ends of both sides, chisel out the waste in the same manner as with the drawer back.

10. THEY'RE USUALLY RIGHT ON, but if they're not, it's not a problem. Klausz cuts small wedges from an offcut of the same board that the flawed dovetail was cut from. He tapers the wedge in two planes so that as it's tapped into the gap between pin and tail, it closes up tightly both on the end and on the side. By using the same wood, you get an almost invisible repair.

Fitting
a Drawer

BY ALAN PETERS

My wife, Laura, doesn't understand why I make such a fuss about drawer fitting. The drawers in our kitchen cabinets slide on plastic runners, and she says they work better than the drawers in any of my furniture. I can't argue with that—those nylon rollers do their job well. But plastic slides don't belong on dovetailed drawers. Fine furniture

requires another solution, an approach that substitutes craftsmanship for the manufactured precision of drawer slides.

The technique we use in my workshop involves three successive levels of fitting. The first is of the individual drawer parts, then the assembled drawer without its bottom, and finally, the drawer with its bottom installed. The result is a drawer that fits so

Fitting Drawer Parts

Sides first

1 MARK THE DRAWER SIDES. Because each drawer is fit precisely to a particular opening, the location and orientation of each part is marked.

2 SHOOT THE EDGE. A sharp jointer plane and a shooting board will give you a straight edge that's 90° to the face of the drawer side. A little wax on the sole and side of the plane will help it glide better.

continued on p. 132

well that it's slowed by a cushion of air as you push it in. And when you pull out the drawer, any other drawers in the case are gently pulled back into the nearly airtight case. It takes time to achieve this piston fit, but the results speak for themselves. Other furniture makers may pride themselves on their dovetails or some other joinery, but for me, a finely fitted drawer is the benchmark of a craftsman's skill.

Well-Built Drawers Start with Stable Wood

Drawer sides should only be made of top-quality, mild-grained, and, preferably, quarter-sawn stock. What you are looking for is wood that will remain straight, move very little with shifts in humidity, and plane easily and cleanly. At the top of my list is Honduras mahogany. Most of my drawer sides are made of material salvaged from old, factory-made mahogany furniture. Because of its age, the wood is about as stable as it's ever going to be. After mahogany, quarter-sawn oak is my choice for drawer sides.

I make my choice depending on the wood used for the drawer fronts, always aiming for a contrast in color. I like mahogany with lighter-colored drawer fronts, such as ash or sycamore, and oak sides when the drawer fronts are made of darker woods, such as walnut or rosewood. From time to time, I use other woods, such as teak, because it wears so well, and rippled (curly) sycamore on special cabinets or desks, where the visual quality of the drawer sides is very important.

Fit the Drawer Pieces Individually and Precisely

Regardless of how much care you put into making and fitting the drawer, it will not fit well if the opening in the case is not consistent front to back and top to bottom. Check the openings, and true them with a shoulder plane if necessary. Make sure, above all, that the case doesn't taper in from

Fitting Drawer Parts

3 SNUG BUT NOT BINDING. When the sides will just slide in and out without binding in the case, they're fit. If they do bind, look for shiny spots on the top edge, which indicate high spots.

front to back. Once the case is trued up, sand the inside, and polish it with a good-quality paste wax.

I don't make or fit drawers on damp or particularly humid days. Instead, I'll wait for a dry spell so that the drawer parts aren't swollen with moisture. Also, whenever possible, I bring the drawer stock into the shop to acclimate for a few weeks before dimensioning it.

Fit the sides first, top to bottom The first step in fitting the drawer pieces is to cut them to rough size, say, within ⅛ in. of finished length and width. All pieces can be thicknessed to final dimension, as long as you bear in mind that you'll be planing and sanding them slightly to fit. Before I do any planing, I use a pair of winding sticks to be sure that all pieces are flat.

I work with the sides first, testing both faces of each side to see which planes better. I choose this side for the face because it will have to be planed to fit and mark it accordingly. If there's more than one drawer, I also indicate which drawer the part belongs to. The end of the drawer where I start my plane stroke becomes the front end so that all fitting is from front to back. If one edge of a drawer side is more difficult to plane, I try to make it the bottom edge because the top edge is where all the planing to fit takes place. Then I plane the inside of the drawer and sand it with 400-grit paper. After this, I shouldn't have to do anything more other than apply a coat of paste wax.

I cut the sides to length on the table saw and then plane the bottom edges on a shooting board. I saw the other edges to within ⅟₁₆ in. of the finished width (or less) and then plane them, too, on the shooting board. After nearly every pass with the plane, I check the fit in the case. If it binds, I check the top edge to see where it's burnished, indicating rubbing between the drawer side and the case, and remove a shaving there. When the side goes all the

THE SIDES HAVE BEEN FITTED. The drawer backs are next. Colored dots at the corners of the case piece identify mating edges and indicate the front of the case.

way home without binding, but still requires a fair amount of force, it's ready. There should be no play at all. Further fitting, which will make the drawer side move more freely, will take place after the drawer has been assembled. Repeat the process for all drawer sides in the case.

Fit the back perfectly A perfect fit for the back is absolutely essential because it is used as the pattern for the front. With large drawers, I fit each back precisely to its opening, so it just snugs into the case opening on all four sides. This is important because the opening often will not be perfectly square. Fitting the back (and then front) of the drawer to the opening helps to ensure a perfect fit.

On small drawers, however, like the ones in this desktop unit, it's less important to fit the drawer backs from top to bottom. Because the drawers are so narrow, only the lengths of the backs need to be fit to the case openings. Openings this small can't be out of square by very much.

Fitting Drawer Parts

Drawer backs are next

FIT THE BACKS FROM SIDE TO SIDE.
Check the fit often because only one
stroke of the plane separates a drawer
that fits from one that's sloppy. These
drawer backs have been cut to width
to fit over drawer bottoms.

FRONTS ARE FITTED. With all drawer parts fit to their openings, the drawers can
now be dovetailed together.

I mark the backs by indicating which
drawer each one belongs to and writing
this number on a little round paper dot that
I can peel off later. I stick the dot on the
inside of the drawer—facing the front of
the cabinet, at the top—so I know how the
back is supposed to be oriented throughout
the fitting process.

To prepare the back, I shoot the bottom
edge and then saw and plane the top edge
to width to fit snugly in the drawer opening. Then I'll transfer the outline of the
drawer back to the front before cutting the
back to width to fit over the drawer bottom, which slides beneath it. In the case of
a small drawer, though, I just cut and plane
the back to width right away. I get this
measurement—from the top of the drawer
bottom groove to the top of the opening—
from my full-scale drawing.

Next, I shoot one end of the back
square, set it in place in the opening, and

then position the other end as closely as possible to where it belongs. I make a pencil mark at this end, cut the back just a hair long, and then plane it to fit, checking it in the case after each stroke.

To prevent end-grain tearout at the edge of the board (what we call spelching here in England), I pivot the plane nearly 90° to the direction of cut as I complete the stroke. This way, the blade cuts across the fibers at the edge of the board rather than catching them and breaking them off. There should be no gap at all at the ends of the backs when they're in place in the case.

The front should fit like a plug I mark out the length of the front by placing the corresponding back on it, with the bottom edges flush, and knifing marks at either end of the back. After shooting the bottom edge of the front, I saw and then plane the top edge to fit, beveling it ever so slightly front to back. I check the fit after each stroke, holding the piece in its opening at an angle (because it hasn't been cut to length yet), being extremely careful not to take off too much with any one pass.

I fit the front from end to end in the same way that I do the back, except that I bevel the ends slightly, just like the top. The front should fit its opening exactly, with no gaps around it at all.

Fitting the Drawer Box

Drawer joinery is another subject entirely—far too big to include in this article. Suffice it to say that any drawer worth fitting this well has been properly dovetailed. And be sure to mark out the dovetails so the tails stand slightly proud of the pins. The front and back of each drawer have been fitted precisely to the opening, so you'll want to remove material from the drawer sides, not from the ends of the front or back, which are your reference lengths.

When I glue up a dovetailed drawer, I don't use any clamps, relying instead on the accuracy of the joints to hold the drawer

Fitting Drawer Parts

Drawer fronts are last

1 MARK THE FRONTS FROM THE BACKS. **Because the backs fit snugly from end to end (and on large drawers, from top to bottom), they can be used to lay out the fronts. Marking with a knife gives the author a precise line that he extends across the face of the drawer front with a small square.**

2 PLANE A SLIGHT BEVEL ON THE ENDS. **This inward taper helps with the fitting of the drawer front.**

3 FITTING THE FRONTS. **With the fronts snugged into place, no light or gaps should be visible at the top, bottom, or sides.**

Fitting Drawers to the Case

Make it square

MAKE SURE THE DRAWER GLUES UP SQUARE. As soon as the joints are together, compare diagonals and adjust the drawer box if necessary.

together. I use glue very sparingly and just tap the dovetails home with a hammer. I use a block of wood to prevent the surface of the drawer sides from being marred. The same goes for mortises and tenons, which I sometimes use to attach the back to the sides as I did on this drawer. Extending the sides past the back allows the drawer to open fully without dropping out of its opening. Whatever the construction, if a drawer is going to fit its opening well, it's important to compare measurements from corner to corner when gluing up and to make adjustments to get the drawer square.

A drawer board supports the drawer as you plane Once the glue has cured (I wait several hours at least, but overnight is better), I take a chisel and pare away the top back corner of both sides. If the back corner was dovetailed, often it will have swollen up because of the moisture introduced by the glue. Even if that's not the case, taking down

this corner will prevent the drawer from binding as it enters the case. I also ease all the arrises (the sharp corners where edge meets side) with a block plane followed by some fine sandpaper, and I soften the top edge of the drawer back.

I leave the bottom out at this stage so I can position the drawer over a drawer board to plane the sides. The drawer board fully supports the drawer but doesn't get in the way of the plane. The drawer board should fit quite accurately between the inside faces of the drawer front and back.

I take a few passes with a plane to bring the sides flush with the end grain of the drawer front and back and then check the fit of the drawer in its opening. I leave just a little sanding or planing to do after the drawer bottom is installed. I slide the drawer in and out of its opening rapidly a few times. This burnishes the sides and top edges of the drawer sides wherever they're rubbing

Fitting Drawers to the Case

Trim to fit

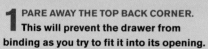

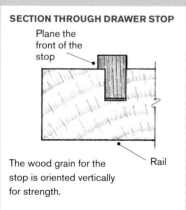

2 CLEAN UP THE SIDES. A few strokes with a plane will bring the sides flush with the end grain of the front and back, which have been fit precisely and should not be planed further.

1 PARE AWAY THE TOP BACK CORNER. This will prevent the drawer from binding as you try to fit it into its opening.

SECTION THROUGH DRAWER STOP

Plane the front of the stop

The wood grain for the stop is oriented vertically for strength.

Rail

3 PLANE STOPS TO POSITION DRAWER FRONT. If you have more than one drawer stop per drawer, remove material evenly from each.

against the case. I plane away these burnished (shiny) spots and check the fit again.

This process is repeated until the drawer will move in and out with relative ease but no slop. The closer I get to a fit, the more often I check. As you're planing the drawer sides, be careful not to remove too much

material from the edge of the drawer front, where it would be visible from the front of the case. After cleaning up the dovetails, I often won't touch this area with a plane again. I just sand it lightly until the fit is right.

Final fit is with the drawer bottom in place Once the drawer is sliding nicely in its opening, it's time to put the drawer bottom in. I almost always use solid cedar of Lebanon. It smells nice, my clients like it, and it keeps moths and worms away. Because it's solid wood, I orient the grain from side to side so that any expansion is front to back. I spot-glue the bottom at the front so that no gap opens up there, and I screw the bottom to the back using slotted screw holes so the bottom can move.

To make sure that the bottom is seated in its groove all the way along its length, I set the drawer on the bench on one side and then tap on the other with a hammer. A piece of scrap protects the side that's being hammered. I repeat the process on the other side.

Next, I check the fit of the drawer in its opening. Often it will need no further fitting. If it's a little snug, removing a shaving or two is the most that will be necessary. A light sanding with 400 grit usually will do.

With the drawer fit, I make sure all outer faces and edges are sanded to 400 grit (the insides have already been done). Then I apply a coat of paste wax to all surfaces except the face of the drawer front. It will be finished with the case later.

Drawer Stop Determines the Position of the Front

All that remains is to get the plane of the drawer front where you want it—either flush with the sides of the case or back a bit if you prefer. Many furniture makers simply glue a small block of wood to the drawer divider for a drawer stop, perhaps affixing a piece of leather or felt to cushion the impact. Unfortunately, this type of drawer stop will almost always get knocked out over time.

In my shop, we prevent this problem by mortising L-shaped drawer stops into the drawer dividers (mortises are cut before the case is assembled). The grain of the drawer stop is oriented vertically, perpendicular to the dividers. No amount of force will break off a stop like this, and the leg of the L-shape gives me material to plane away to get the drawer to stop where I want it. I check the drawer in its opening once more, this time to see how much material I must remove from the front of the stop. A few passes with a bullnose plane and the job is done. If you have more than one stop (I usually use two, one near either case side), try to remove material evenly from both stops. To see if you've succeeded, place a little pressure against the drawer front right in front of one of the stops. If the drawer front gives at all, the stop behind it has had more material removed from it. The other one will need a shaving or two removed to even things up. As always, the closer I get to where I want to be, the more cautiously I proceed.

ALAN PETERS first began woodworking as an apprentice in Edward Barnsley's workshop in 1949. He has been designing and building furniture ever since. In 1990, he received the OBE (Order of the British Empire) from the queen of England in recognition of his contributions as a designer and craftsman. He lives and works in Kentisbeare, Devon, England, where he manages a team of four other craftsmen.

THE RESULT IS A DRAWER THAT FITS SO WELL it's slowed by a cushion of air as you push it in. And when you pull out the drawer, any other drawers in the case are gently pulled back into the nearly airtight case.

Versatile Plywood Drawers

BY GARY ROGOWSKI

PERFECT FOR HIDING all the clutter around your house and shop, plywood drawers also are simple to build.

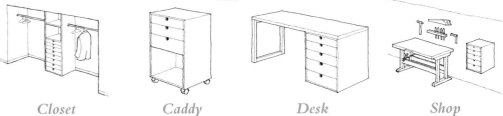

Closet *Caddy* *Desk* *Shop*

Some drawers are built with great care, hinting at the treasures hiding behind their polished faces. They have the look and feel of a crisply tailored suit. But plywood utility drawers feel more like loose-fitting jeans: They're made for comfort and use, not for show. Utility drawers are the perfect receptacles for those minor tornadoes of odds and ends.

You can build simple plywood drawers using a table saw, a router, and your choice of two basic joints: the rabbet or the tongue and dado. For ease of construction, build the drawers with ½-in. plywood (I use 9-ply Baltic birch) or a high-density particleboard. Just make sure your sheet goods are flat and of consistent thickness. Millwork then simply involves cutting the parts to length and width. Use ¼-in. plywood for the drawer bottoms, which also serve as the drawer runners.

Building a
Spline-Mitered Box

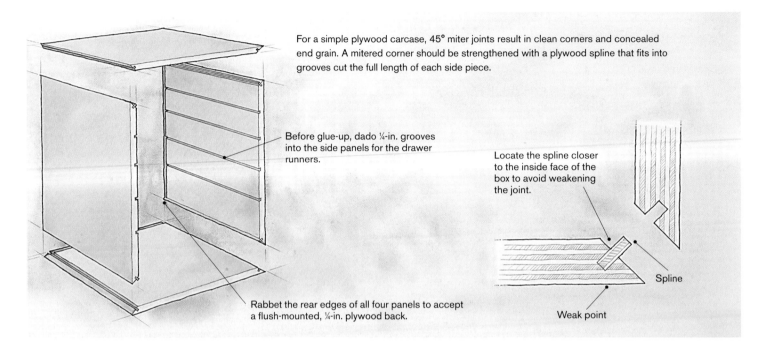

For a simple plywood carcase, 45° miter joints result in clean corners and concealed end grain. A mitered corner should be strengthened with a plywood spline that fits into grooves cut the full length of each side piece.

Before glue-up, dado ¼-in. grooves into the side panels for the drawer runners.

Locate the spline closer to the inside face of the box to avoid weakening the joint.

Spline

Weak point

Rabbet the rear edges of all four panels to accept a flush-mounted, ¼-in. plywood back.

Construct the cabinet carcase out of the same ½-in. plywood used for the drawers. For a clean look, I spline-miter my cabinet sides together, as shown in the drawing above. I rabbet the rear edges to accept a flush-mounted, ¼-in. plywood back, but you could rabbet the sides together and simply screw on the back. Before glue-up, dado ¼-in.-wide grooves into the cabinet sides for the drawer runners to rest in. Make sure the case goes together square by checking the diagonals across the face and back of the cabinet. Pull the cabinet square by clamping across the longer diagonal. Squaring the cabinet will make fitting the drawers much simpler later on.

Both the rabbet and the tongue and dado are excellent joints for plywood construction because they help line up the drawer parts when gluing. The difference between these joints is partly structural and partly visual. The tongue and dado shows the ply edge on the face of the drawer, whereas the rabbet keeps this edge hidden

from sight. But the rabbet needs fasteners such as dowels or nails to resist being pulled apart every time the drawer is yanked open. Because the tongue of the drawer front is secured by the dado of the drawer side, the tongue and dado naturally resists this same movement.

You can cut either joint on a router table (see the sidebars on the facing page and on p. 142). For pulls, I bore 1-in. holes in the drawer fronts with a Multispur bit or a Forstner bit, positioning the bit so that a portion of the hole overlaps the top edge of the drawer.

Glue up the drawer sides, and then glue on the bottoms. Make sure that the drawer boxes fit between the case sides with only a little slop; let the drawer bottom be the item you adjust for that perfect fit. Then comes the best moment: filling all those drawers with stuff.

GARY ROGOWSKI is a contributing editor to *Fine Woodworking* magazine.

The Tongue-and-Dado Joint

The simplest setup for cutting a tongue-and-dado joint requires only one bit-height setting on the router table. However, the bit hole in the table must be small enough or have a table
insert to prevent the drawer pieces from diving into the hole
when passed vertically over it. If your table doesn't have an insert,
drill an access hole through some flat ¼-in. plywood or hardboard,
and clamp it to your table.

FIRST, CUT THE DADOES IN THE DRAWER SIDES. The dado should be one-third (or less) the thickness of the board.

First, cut the dadoes in the drawer sides. Set the bit height for
the full dado cut, and then position and clamp the fence. I always
take a practice pass before committing good stock to the cut. If
the dado is in the right place, the outside face of the drawer front
will wind up flush with the end of the drawer side. Without
changing the bit-depth setting, cut the tongues in the drawer face
and back with the pieces held vertically. Score the face with a
gauge line to prevent tearout. You will have to adjust the fence to
get a perfect-fitting tongue.

Because the end of the dado is fragile and can break off, avoid
too tight a fit, and use caution when pulling the joint apart.

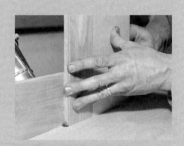

NEXT, CUT THE TONGUES IN THE DRAWER FACE AND BACK. Adjust the fence for the shoulder width, but leave the bit height the same as it was for the dadoes. Hold the stock vertically.

TEST THE FIT. If you cut the dado first and use it to locate the tongue, the fit should be right.

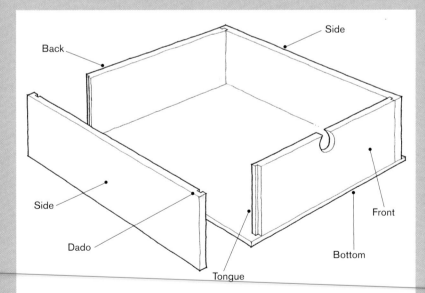

Back

Side

Side

Dado

Tongue

Front

Bottom

The Rabbet Joint

The rabbet joint requires just one router cut in-to each end of the drawer face and back. The drawer sides are simply crosscut to the correct length, figured by taking the outside dimension of the drawer box less the width of the rabbet on both ends. Use a router bit the same width as the drawer side, so you can cut the full width of the rabbet with each pass across the bit.

To spare your bit, take two separate passes to cut the rabbets to depth. The first pass takes away about ⅛ in. of material; the second cuts to depth, in this case, ¼ in. A rabbet joint can also be roughed out on a saw and then router-cut in only one pass, with the bit set to full depth.

The sides on my utility drawers are about 3 in. wide. When you cut narrow boards like these on a router table, you can gang up two or three to give them greater stability against the fence and to re-duce tearout. Make sure you're aware of where your fingers are when the bit emerges from the cut. After the drawers are glued up, pin the drawer sides to the face and back with ⅛-in. dowel pins. If you prefer to fasten the sides with finish nails, drive the nails at a slight inward angle, and set the nail heads.

GANG SEVERAL PIECES TOGETHER. Cutting two or three pieces at once improves stability against the fence and reduces tearout.

PIN A RABBET JOINT WITH DOWELS OR NAILS. Fasteners keep the joint from breaking apart when the drawer is yanked open.

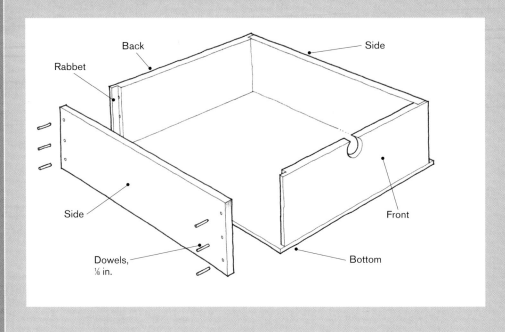

Back

Rabbet

Side

Side

Front

Dowels, ⅛ in.

Bottom

A Better Way to Build Drawers

BY MARK EDMUNDSON

onsider a dresser drawer that is 16 in. deep and 30 in. wide. Let's say that every time it's opened it travels 12 in. out and 12 in. back in. If this drawer is opened once a day for 30 years, it will have traveled more than four miles, carrying its load of sweaters and jeans solely on the thickness of the drawer sides. By then it's probably running like a brick over

a cheese grater. Worse, if the wear extends into the groove for the drawer bottom, it will damage not only the drawer but also the carcase itself.

Side-hung drawers avoid this problem by having the drawer run on rails dadoed into the drawer sides. French bottoms avoid

The NK Advantage

Traditional drawer

Thin, tall sides create a large friction surface area and are prone to sticking. Narrow glide surfaces wear out quickly.

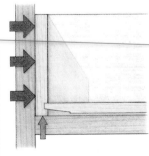

NK drawer

Short, wide runners in the bottom assembly reduce the friction area and provide a wide, long-wearing glide surface.

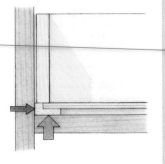

NK DRAWERS, named for the Swedish furniture manufacturer that popularized them, use a separate bottom assembly to eliminate the drawbacks of standard drawer designs.

the wear by adding slips to the bottom of the sides, which increase the surface that bears the weight of the drawer. In both of these cases, however, the sides still rub against the drawer opening. This is especially a problem in deep drawers, where the tall sides are difficult to fit to the carcase and are prone to sticking.

A style that solves both problems—excessive wear and too much friction—is the NK (pronounced "enco") drawer, developed in the early 1900s by a Swedish manufacturer, Nordiska Kompaniet. I started building NK drawers, which require no hardware, for deep drawers. Now I make almost all of my drawers this way.

The NK drawer is quite different from a standard drawer. For one, the front is slightly

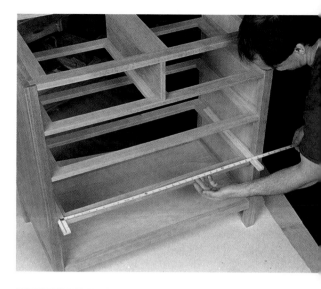

START WITH THE BOTTOM ASSEMBLY. With the runners in place, determine the width of the plywood bottom. Cut the bottom a bit wider than necessary. Then trim it to fit.

Build the Bottom, Then the Box

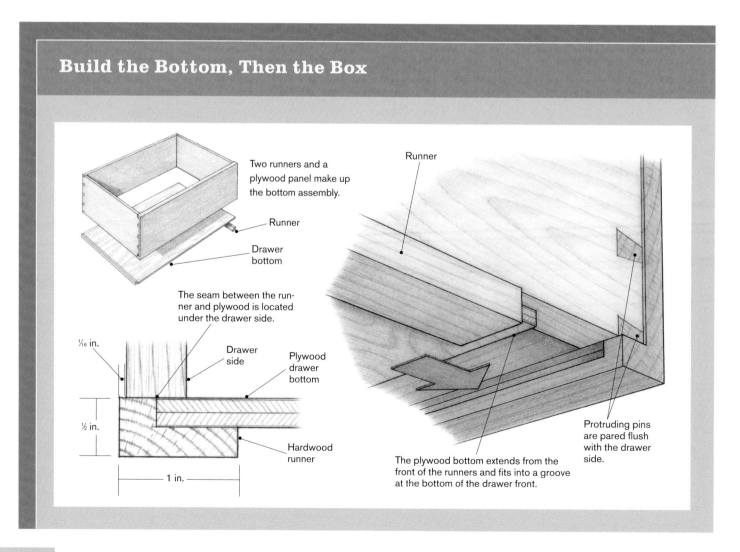

Two runners and a plywood panel make up the bottom assembly.

Runner

Drawer bottom

Runner

The seam between the runner and plywood is located under the drawer side.

¹⁄₁₆ in.

Drawer side

Plywood drawer bottom

½ in.

Hardwood runner

1 in.

Protruding pins are pared flush with the drawer side.

The plywood bottom extends from the front of the runners and fits into a groove at the bottom of the drawer front.

wider than the sides, except where the dovetail pins have been pared flush. Runners glued to the bottom of the sides also protrude from the sides, making them even with the sides of the drawer front. The last big difference is the bottom. It's made of plywood and glued into a rabbet in each runner.

The NK drawer has a few advantages over a standard drawer. The runners provide extra surface area where it's needed—under the drawer—and reduce the amount of surface area rubbing at the sides. Also, fitting this drawer means fitting the bottom assembly only, which is easier than fitting a standard drawer, especially if it is large. Without the front, sides, and back of the drawer to obstruct your view, it's easy to see where the runners are binding. Finally, even if the box isn't glued up perfectly square, the drawer will operate smoothly because the bottom sits proud of the sides.

Build the Bottom Assembly First

The construction of the NK drawer is as different as its design. The bottom assembly comes first because it determines the dimensions of the drawer box. The bottom assembly is composed of three parts: two runners and a plywood bottom. Fine plywoods are available in a variety of species, but I often make my own drawer bottoms with veneer chosen to match the drawer front, laid up on a thin plywood core.

The runner dimensions must be sized to minimize the friction against the carcase sides and maximize the support of the drawer's weight. On the dresser featured here, the drawers are 16 in. deep and 30 in. wide, with heights ranging from 5¾ in. to 8 in. I made the runners ½ in. high and 1 in. wide.

THE DRAWER POCKET IS THE BEST PLACE FOR GLUING UP THE BOTTOM ASSEMBLY. **The author uses clamping cauls and small sticks wedged against the drawer divider above.**

Because the runners butt up to the drawer front, their lengths are determined by subtracting the thickness of the drawer front from the drawer depth. In this case, the front is ¾ in. thick, so the runner length is 15¼ in. The runners are rabbeted to accept the bottom. The rabbet depth is the same as the thickness of the bottom, and the width of the rabbet is such that the edge of the plywood will end up directly underneath the drawer side, splitting its thickness. Because the runners provide all of the support for the drawer, the drawer sides can be thinner than ½ in. For these large drawers, I resawed 5/4 stock and ended up with sides that are ½ in. thick.

Once the runners have been rabbeted, place them into the drawer opening and measure the distance between the walls of the rabbets. Cut the plywood panel a hair wider so that you have some wood to work with when making the final fit. You may want to glue a strip of solid wood to the back edge of the plywood to conceal the core. The bottom must extend past the front of the runners into a groove in the drawer front, so make the bottom ¼ in.

longer than the runners. Once these pieces have been cut to size but before gluing them together, test the fit in the drawer opening. If the fit is tight, you shouldn't have too much work to make it run smoothly, but if it won't fit at all, reduce the width of the bottom. If it's too loose, place a shim between the plywood's edge and the rabbet during glue-up. Once these pieces are to your liking, they may be glued up.

The bottom assembly may also be glued up in the drawer pocket itself, to ensure a close fit from the get-go. This way you also can align the front edges of the runners with the carcase during glue-up, which in turn will cause the drawer front to be parallel with the front of the carcase. You will need two ¼-in.-square clamping cauls cut to the same length as the runners. Place the bottom assembly in the drawer pocket and set the cauls on the outside edges of the plywood. The easiest way to clamp down the cauls is to wedge small sticks against the drawer divider above. Make sure that the back of the runners and the back of the bottom remain flush.

When the glue is dry, you can begin fitting the bottom assembly to the drawer pocket. This definitely will be the easiest large drawer that you will ever fit. The bottom assembly should fit the pocket tightly and only need a few plane strokes to make it run smoothly, but there is always at least one renegade in the bunch that will need a little bit more coaxing. Begin by flipping the assembly upside down and fitting the front few inches of it into the opening. If the back is still off, check the dimension of the back end of the bottom, fitting from the back of the cabinet. Once this is done, plane the runners so they are once again straight. Check the fit frequently to avoid removing too much material.

To test whether the bottom assembly fits and is running smoothly, pull it out about three-quarters of the way (you may have to place a weight at the back of the assembly to keep it from tipping) and try to close it by pressing at either the right side or the left side. If the assembly goes in without binding, it's ready. If it sticks, it probably needs a little bit of sanding to create a smoother run.

If, in the excitement of fitting the bottom assembly, you take off a little too much wood—which I've done more than once— and the fit becomes sloppy, just rip about ⅛ in. off the side of the runner, glue on a slightly thicker strip, and start again.

The runners must line up evenly with the front of the opening to ensure a consistent reveal around the drawer front. If the runners don't line up, use the front of the carcase to determine how much to trim the longer runner. Scribe a line and clamp a square guide block to the runner, then pare away the excess with a chisel.

EACH PART DETERMINES THE SIZE OF THE NEXT ONE. **Lay out the groove in the drawer front directly from the bottom assembly. Then measure to the groove in the drawer front to determine the height of the drawer sides.**

Dry-Fit and Measure for Sides and Back

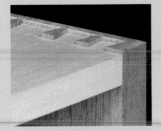

THE DRAWER SIDE IS SET IN FROM THE BOTTOM RUNNERS AND THE SIDES OF THE DRAWER FRONT. When laying out the half-blind pins, set a marking gauge about 1⁄16 in. heavier than the thickness of the drawer sides.

TEMPORARILY ATTACH THE BOTTOM ASSEMBLY TO FIND YOUR NEXT DIMENSIONS. Use the back of the drawer runners to scribe the length of the sides.

Size the Drawer Front

Cut and plane down the edges of the drawer front until the drawer fits snugly in the carcase opening. Using the bottom assembly as a reference, locate the groove in the drawer front that will receive the protruding edge of the plywood.

Now measure from the top of the drawer front to the top of the groove to find the height of the drawer sides. Add a fraction more to the height to allow for slight misalignment of dovetails.

Cut the half-blind dovetails

Cut the tails first. Then, to hold the sides in from the runners and the drawer front, set a marking gauge 1⁄16 in. heavier than the drawer side's thickness when laying out the pins in the drawer front. Any more than 1⁄16 in., and the drawer front's protruding end grain will be too fragile.

I leave the sides long until I've finished the joinery at the front. This way, if I mess

up a set of tails, I can cut them off and do them over again. Usually I cut all of the pins in the fronts, choose the worst-fitting side, and redo its tails, working in reverse and marking from pins to tails. This second chance takes a little pressure off cutting dovetails.

After the joinery has been cut for the sides and fronts, dry-fit the parts and place the box on top of the bottom assembly. If everything looks good and the runners are snug against the drawer front, use the runners to mark off the lengths of the sides. Then cut the sides to length.

Now measure the distance from the outside of one drawer side to the outside of the other at the front, and cut the back to that dimension. After the joinery has been completed but before the glue-up, finish-sand the drawer sides; otherwise, the protruding runners and drawer front will make sanding difficult.

Pare the Pins After Assembly

A SMALL DOWEL AT THE BACK HELPS KEEP THE DRAWER BOX ALIGNED DURING GLUE-UP. Just be sure that the edges of the drawer front line up exactly with the sides of the runners.

PARING BACK THE PINS. Use a small stack of index cards and a plane blade to pare away the pins without tearing out the short grain. Remove one card at a time until they're gone and the pins are trimmed flush. Sections of the half-pins at the top and bottom are removed, leaving them square.

Glue Up the Drawer

Gluing up an NK drawer can be a bit fussy. Start by gluing up the front, sides, and back. Once that assembly is dry, you're ready to attach the bottom assembly. Line up the sides and runners carefully: If the front overhangs a runner on one side, it will come up too short on the other, and all could be lost.

The back corners of the drawer should be centered on the bottom assembly. To ensure alignment, while the assembly is clamped up during the dry-fitting, drill a small hole at the back of the plywood bottom, up into the drawer back. During glue-up, slide a dowel into this hole. The front will stay put because the plywood bottom slides into the groove in the drawer front.

All that's left now is to pare down the protruding pins on the drawer front. A sharp chisel will do, but I like to use a freshly sharpened plane blade and some index cards as shims. If you take off too much at once, the end grain can crumble. Start with a stack of index cards slightly lower than the pins, lay down the blade, and make small shearing cuts. Then remove a card or two and repeat as necessary. Finally, pare away the slope of the half-pins at the top and bottom, leaving horizontal lines.

NK drawers are more complex than standard drawers, but they make fitting large drawers a much less nerve-wracking job. And it's a comfort to know that these drawers will continue to run smoothly as the years and miles pile up.

MARK EDMUNDSON is a furniture maker in northern Idaho.

Credits

The articles in this book appeared in the following issues of *Fine Woodworking*:

p. 4: Making Big Cabinets Manageable by Niall Barrett, issue 122. Photos by William Duckworth, courtesy *Fine Woodworking*, © The Taunton Press, Inc.

p. 9: A Game Plan for Big Cabinet Jobs by John W. West, issue 127. Photos by William Duckworth, courtesy *Fine Woodworking*, © The Taunton Press, Inc.; Drawings by Christopher Clapp, courtesy *Fine Woodworking*, © The Taunton Press, Inc.

p. 18: Cabinets Built for the Long Haul by Bill Crozier, issue 136. Photos by Jefferson Kolle, courtesy *Fine Woodworking*, © The Taunton Press, Inc. except photos on p. 24 by Bill Crozier, courtesy *Fine Woodworking*, © The Taunton Press, Inc.; Drawings by Bill Moser, courtesy *Fine Woodworking*, © The Taunton Press, Inc.

p. 25: Extraordinary Built-Ins by Ross Day, issue 149. Photos by Anatole Burkin, courtesy *Fine Woodworking*, © The Taunton Press, Inc.; Drawings by Michael Gellatly, courtesy *Fine Woodworking*, © The Taunton Press, Inc.

p. 32: A Woodworker's Guide to Medium-Density Fiberboard by Jim Hayden, issue 104. Photos by William Sampson, courtesy *Fine Woodworking*, © The Taunton Press, Inc. except photos on p. 34 by Jim Hayden, courtesy *Fine Woodworking*, © The Taunton Press, Inc.

P. 40: Working with Synthetic Countertop Materials by Ken Piccou, issue 108. Photos by Vincent Laurence, courtesy *Fine Woodworking*, © The Taunton Press, Inc. except photo on p. 40 by Robert Marsala, courtesy *Fine Woodworking*, © The Taunton Press, Inc.

p. 46: No-Hassle Panel Handling by Skip Lauderbaugh, issue 114. Photos by Alec Waters, courtesy *Fine Woodworking*, © The Taunton Press, Inc.

p. 50: Paint-Grade Cabinets by Lars Mikklesen, issue 103. Photos by Sandor Nagyszalanczy, courtesy *Fine Woodworking*, © The Taunton Press, Inc.; Drawings by Rob Mihaley, courtesy *Fine Woodworking*, © The Taunton Press, Inc.

p. 58: Solid-Wood Edging for Plywood by Steven Cook, issue 116. Photos by Graham Ashford, courtesy *Fine Woodworking*, © The Taunton Press, Inc.

p. 61: Dressing Up Plywood Cabinets with Face Frames by Joseph Beals, issue 128. Photos by Strother Purdy, courtesy *Fine Woodworking*, © The Taunton Press, Inc.; Drawings by Tim Langenderfer, courtesy *Fine Woodworking*, © The Taunton Press, Inc.

p. 68: Fine Furniture from Plywood by Mark Edmundson, issue 157. Photos by Asa Christiana, courtesy *Fine Woodworking*, © The Taunton Press, Inc. except top left and right photos on p. 76 by Michael Pekovich, courtesy *Fine Woodworking*, © The Taunton Press, Inc.; Drawings by Vince Babak, courtesy *Fine Woodworking*, © The Taunton Press, Inc.

p. 79: Six Ways to Edge Plywood by Mario Rodriguez, issue 156. Photos by William Duckworth, courtesy *Fine Woodworking*, © The Taunton Press, Inc. except for photo on p. 79 by Kelly J. Dunton, courtesy *Fine Woodworking*, © The Taunton Press, Inc.; Drawings by Vince Babak, courtesy *Fine Woodworking*, © The Taunton Press, Inc.

p. 86: Frame-and-Panel Doors: An Illustrated Guide by Graham Blackburn, issue 129. Drawings by Graham Blackburn, courtesy *Fine Woodworking*, © The Taunton Press, Inc.

p.92: Three Ways to Make Cabinet Doors by Steve Latta, issue 135. Photos by Anatole Burkin, courtesy *Fine Woodworking*, © The Taunton Press, Inc. except for photos on p. 92-93 (top), p. 95 (bottom) and p. 98 by Michael Pekovich, courtesy *Fine Woodworking*, © The Taunton Press, Inc.

p. 99: Quick but Sturdy Cabinet Door by Mario Rodriguez, issue 104. Photos by Jonathan Binzen, courtesy *Fine Woodworking*, © The Taunton Press, Inc.; Drawing by Heather Lambert, courtesy *Fine Woodworking*, © The Taunton Press, Inc.

p. 102: Fitting Flush-Mounted Doors by Steven Thomas Bunn, issue 107. Photos by Charley Robinson, courtesy *Fine Woodworking*, © The Taunton Press, Inc.; Drawings courtesy *Fine Woodworking*, © The Taunton Press, Inc.

p. 109: Glazing Cabinet Doors by Tony Konovaloff, issue 116. Photos by Aimé Fraser, courtesy *Fine Woodworking*, © The Taunton Press, Inc.; Drawings by Vince Babak, courtesy *Fine Woodworking*, © The Taunton Press, Inc.

p. 115: Arched Top Cabinet Doors by Bill Ewing, issue 138. Photos by Matthew Teague, courtesy *Fine Woodworking*, © The Taunton Press, Inc.; Drawings by Jim Richey, courtesy *Fine Woodworking*, © The Taunton Press, Inc.

p. 122: Smooth Tambours by Mike Weiss, issue 150. Photos by Mark Schofield, courtesy *Fine Woodworking*, © The Taunton Press, Inc.; Drawings by Vince Babak, courtesy *Fine Woodworking*, © The Taunton Press, Inc.

p. 127: Making a Drawer with Half-Blind Dovetails by Frank Klausz, issue 100. Photos by Sandor Nagyszalanczy, courtesy *Fine Woodworking*, © The Taunton Press, Inc. except photos p. 128 (right top and bottom) by Vincent Laurence, courtesy *Fine Woodworking*, © The Taunton Press, Inc.; Drawings courtesy *Fine Woodworking*, © The Taunton Press, Inc.

p. 131: Fitting a Drawer by Alan Peters, issue 137. Photos by Vincent Laurence, courtesy *Fine Woodworking*, © The Taunton Press, Inc.

p. 139: Versatile Plywood Drawers by Gary Rogowski, issue 131. Photos by Marc Vassallo, courtesy *Fine Woodworking*, © The Taunton Press, Inc. except photo on p. 139 by Vincent Laurence, courtesy *Fine Woodworking*, © The Taunton Press, Inc.; Drawings by Jim Richey, courtesy *Fine Woodworking*, © The Taunton Press, Inc.

p. 143: A Better Way to Build Drawers by Mark Edmundson, issue 150. Photos by Asa Christiana, courtesy *Fine Woodworking*, © The Taunton Press, Inc.; Drawings by Vince Babak, courtesy *Fine Woodworking*, © The Taunton Press, Inc.

Index

The New Best of Fine Woodworking series

A collection of the best articles from the last ten years of Fine Woodworking.

OTHER BOOKS IN THE SERIES

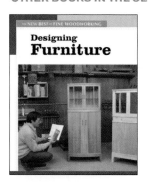

Designing Furniture
The New Best of
Fine Woodworking
From the editors of FWW
ISBN 1-56158-684-6
Product #070767
$17.95

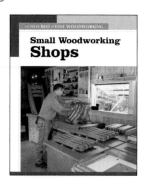

Small Woodworking Shops
The New Best of
Fine Woodworking
From the editors of FWW
ISBN 1-56158-686-2
Product #070768
$17.95

Working with Routers
The New Best of
Fine Woodworking
From the editors of FWW
ISBN 1-56158-685-4
Product #070769
$17.95

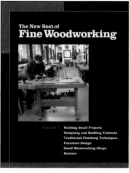

The New Best of Fine Woodworking Slipcase Set Volume 1

Designing Furniture
Working with Routers
Small Woodworking Shops
Designing and Building Cabinets
Building Small Projects
Traditional Finishing Techniques

From the editors of FWW
ISBN 1-56158-736-2
Product #070808
$85.00

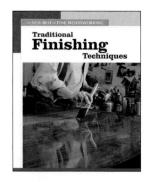

Traditional Finishing Techniques
The New Best of
Fine Woodworking
From the editors of FWW
1-56158-733-8
Product #070793
$17.95

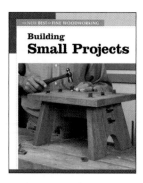

Building Small Projects
The New Best of
Fine Woodworking
From the editors of FWW
ISBN 1-56158-684-6
Product #070767
$17.95